THE CASE
for
CHRIST'S
RESURRECTION

THE CASE
for
CHRIST'S
RESURRECTION

David W. Balsiger
and
Michael Minor

Bridge-Logos
Orlando, Florida 32822

Bridge-Logos

Orlando, FL 32822 USA

The Case for Christ's Resurrection
by David W. Balsiger and Michael Minor

Printed in the United States of America.

Library of Congress Catalog Card Number:
2007930148

ISBN: 978-0-88270-410-4

Unless otherwise noted, all Scripture notations are taken
from the *King James Version* (KJV) of the Bible.

G1.316.N.m706.35230

This Book is Dedicated to

Guy Morrell

My Dear Friend of 20 Years and the
Publisher–Inspirational Leader
Behind Bridge-Logos
(1945-2007)

—David W. Balsiger

Monsignor Giuseppe Ghibert

This book is also dedicated with great
respect and esteem to Monsignor Giuseppe
Ghiberti whose selfless efforts to conserve
the Holy Shroud for future generations and
his tireless apostolate of evangelizing with
the Holy Shroud have spread to millions
the Good News of Him Whose Image
is on the Shroud.

—Michael Minor

ACKNOWLEDGEMENTS

The authors wish to express their appreciation to Joseph Meier and Joette Whims for their writing assistance on this book, to Charles Sellier for his consultation, to Marsha Rano and Debra Pursell for their copy editing and proofing of the manuscript, as well as Ann Strauss and Judy Wood for their administrative assistance. Further appreciation is extended to the following Shroud of Turin scholars for without their help, counsel, research, and frequent consultation, this book would never have been possible—Thomas D'Muhala, Dr. Peter Soons, Dame Isabel Piczek, and Dr. Alan and Mary Whanger. Also, we cannot overlook Vance Syphers, Paul Schubert, and Joe Call who financially supported the writing of this book and the TV/DVD production version.

We would be amiss if we did not mention the fine staff at Bridge-Logos who played important roles in this book—Guy Morrell, Steve Becker, Sue Teubner, Wendy Wood, and Elizabeth Nason.

David W. Balsiger
Michael Minor

CONTENTS

APPENDICES

Peter and the other disciple ran to the tomb to see. The other disciple outran Peter and got there first. He stooped and looked in and saw the linen cloth lying there, but he didn't go in. Then Simon Peter arrived and went inside. He also noticed the linen wrappings lying there, while the cloth that had covered Jesus' head was folded up and lying to the side. Then the other disciple also went in, and he saw and believed—for until then they hadn't realized that the Scriptures said he would rise from the dead (John 20: 3–9, NLT).

* * *

Eight days later the disciples were together again, and this time Thomas was with them. The doors were locked; but suddenly, as before, Jesus was standing among them. He said, "Peace be with you." Then he said to Thomas, "Put your finger here and see my hands. Put your hand into the wound in my side. Don't be faithless any longer. Believe!"

"My Lord and my God!" Thomas exclaimed.

Then Jesus told him, "You believe because you have seen me. Blessed are those who haven't seen me and believe anyway" (John 20: 26–29, NLT).

PREFACE

God's universe is like a magnificent tapestry woven by his Omnipotent Hand before the foundations of the world—and he has given us the ability to study his magnificent tapestry—the universe—and discover its secrets. However, some of the big questions of all time have yet to be answered. The nature of time, the creation of the universe, and perhaps even a link to another dimension—can these great riddles of the universe be solved through the lens of the ancient past? Can the Resurrection of Christ give us new insight into the mind of God? Can the imprint of a crucified body on an ancient burial cloth connect our past with our future?

This book will bring you to the threshold of some of today's most stunning scientific discoveries. Images never before seen will reach out from the dust of antiquity and touch your life in ways you never thought possible. In a world where children grow up playing with computers—and calculus is frequently part of the high school curriculum—many of the scientific mysteries of the past are today's commonplace knowledge. Yet even the world's leading scientists would agree that when it comes to understanding the universe we live in and the physical laws that govern it—only precious few threads of this vast tapestry have been deciphered—but these few threads are endlessly intriguing: Einstein's Theory of Relativity; Quantum Mechanics; Particle Physics, all taunt us with the notion that perhaps we can know the unknowable. Yet these studies have only just begun to reveal the intricate interweaving of forces that make up the universe.

A Message for the World

In the late 1970s, scientists developed a computer program that allowed NASA technicians to read the terrain characteristics of distant planets from two-dimensional satellite photographs. But the developers of this amazing device were in for a shock when they were asked to analyze a photograph of something most of them had never heard of—the Shroud of Turin, an ancient burial cloth with the inscribed image of a crucified man. Actually, what they were looking at was a two-dimensional photograph of a two-dimensional artifact, but to everyone's amazement, from somewhere inside this two-dimensional photograph of this two-dimensional artifact emerged three-dimensional information. A photograph of an ancient burial cloth brought scientists face-to-face with the impossible: three-dimensional information was being discovered stored inside an artifact where it could not possibly exist.

Since that time, many more studies have been conducted on this ancient anomaly—some with astounding results. In fact, some scientists believe that the Shroud can uncover mysteries of the universe we had no idea existed.

In 2004, Dame Isabel Piczek, a particle physicist working independently, made a discovery that could change everything we believe about the world. She was examining properties of the Shroud of Turin when she made an amazing discovery. The cloth may be able to show us some elemental facts about matter that could change the way scientists analyze the universe. Is it possible that something as seemingly inconsequential as a tiny fiber from an ancient burial cloth could contain such a message for the entire world? Have new ways of obtaining long-hidden information been discovered? Some scientists now believe the imprint on this ancient physical artifact uniquely identifies not only the artifact itself, but events surrounding the history of that artifact. The particle physicist studying the ancient piece of cloth concluded that it leads us to a mysterious gateway that opens to a completely different world, "an extraordinary world with extraordinary laws."[1]

What is this mysterious gateway? And what are these extraordinary laws that are only now being discovered? Could it be that time, space, and energy interact in a way never before predicted or comprehended? Is there an overarching principle that unites the theory of relativity and quantum physics? Some researchers suggest that if we could discover that unifying principle, we could explain everything about the physical universe. Modern science is now beginning to decode messages that might even be coming from another dimension. How could an ancient cloth be the gateway to this other dimension?

By and large, scientists agree that there is something that produces the order of the universe, but the big problem is that they don't know *who* or *what* that *something* is. Perhaps the Bible gives us the answer. Colossians 1:16, 17 [NLT] states; "Christ is the one through whom God created everything in heaven and earth. He made the things we can see and the things we can't see—kings, kingdoms, rulers, and authorities. Everything has been created through him and for him. He existed before everything else began, and *he holds all creation together*" [emphasis added].

The Bible contends that Jesus is the one who keeps creation—and its physical laws—running so that everything remains in order. Is that difficult to believe? It all hinges on whether or not one believes that his Resurrection is a historical fact.

Is it possible that scientific pursuits about the universe are being exponentially advanced by the information contained in one ancient, earthly, hand-woven piece of cloth—the Shroud of Turin? If the Resurrection of Christ could be proved to be the crowning event of history, then the Shroud is certainly the most important object in history. It may unlock secrets of the universe by giving us a new way of looking at the material world.

How can an awareness of the Resurrection and the Shroud help us understand the meaning of why we're here and where we're going? Is there some deeper understanding that can be gained through all of this scientific study?

Dame Isabel Piczek believes there is. "I sincerely think," she tells us, "that through these studies we will come upon a completely new structure of physics ... maybe even a completely different world."[2]

Be prepared to have your mind stretched. Approach the facts in this book with an open mind, seeking Truth. Test the evidence and see if it holds up to the scrutiny of scientific and logical investigation. See if what is revealed is worthy of changing your world view forever.

Endnotes

1 Dame Isabel Piczek, Notes on the 2005 Dallas Shroud of Turin Conference Paper.
2 Ibid.

ONE

HISTORICAL FACT OR URBAN LEGEND?

Mankind is in pursuit of answers to life's most fundamental questions: Origin—where did we come from? Meaning—why are we here? Morality—how should we live? And Destiny—where we are going? We want our hope of immortality satisfied, our reason for living validated, and we want assurance of something beyond ourselves—something beyond the world around us—something beyond the grave—we want assurance of eternal life.

In Pursuit of Eternal Life

One event in history eclipses all other events in significance and astonishment. This amazing event—someone coming back from the dead—was accomplished by one man who lived on this earth two-thousand years ago. This one man—and this one event—changed history forever—everything from the way mankind thinks, to how he lives, and what he believes—and answers the most basic questions about life, death and eternity:

• This one man had the power to take up his life again after he died;

• This one man was able to tell us what the after-life is like;

• What this one man had to say carries more importance than the words of any other person in history.

Of course, we are referring to the death, burial, and Resurrection of Jesus Christ. But can the Resurrection be proved? This book analyzes the truth or fallacy of the Resurrection from several vantage points:

• Is there quality evidence that would hold up in a court of law?

• How accurate is the record of this event?

• How did Christ's contemporaries view his Resurrection?

• What are the arguments of the skeptics?

But there is one piece of physical proof— evidence that has outlasted time and all the elements for a period of over twenty centuries—that is offered to validate the Resurrection and we will examine it in painstaking detail. This is the venerated antiquity, known as the Shroud of Turin, which contains the image of a tortured naked man—indelibly and forever imprinted on it. Through the centuries, many have believed this piece of precious antiquity to be the actual burial cloth of Jesus of Nazareth. This burial cloth—from all the evidence—survived the death and Resurrection of the living Christ—and bears the proof of that miraculous event on its very fibers. This Shroud, or burial cloth, has been the center of heated scientific controversy for more than a century—a debate that becomes more fascinating with each passing year.

The Crucifixion

The story of the Resurrection begins with the gruesome events that took place on the infamous day in the pages of history we call "Good Friday"—the Day Jesus Christ was crucified. The four Gospels of the New Testament Bible Matthew—Mark, Luke, and John—taken together, provide us with enough detail about Christ's passion to make it easy to imagine what it may have been like to actually witness the most woeful moment in history.

The detailed account of the Passion of Jesus Christ as given in the Gospels tells of the events leading up to his arrest, the so-called trial before the Sanhedrin, his questioning by the Roman rulers Pilate and Herod, the brutal scourgings, and his ultimate Crucifixion and death on the cross. The details of the Roman method of Crucifixion are also well-known (with the naked victim's outstretched wrists nailed to a wooden cross beam and feet nailed to a wooden platform), and it is believed that thousands of Jews were put to death in this manner during the Roman occupation.

Few experts question the validity of Jesus' Crucifixion. The details in the Gospels are a good representation of the medical facts concerning this type of death. It was a barbaric custom that was meant to deter others from committing the same crimes.

But many skeptics don't have the same reaction to his Resurrection. Many historians, scientists, and ordinary people reject the facts of the Resurrection. They claim it's too supernatural to believe.

But if we take the same approach to developing the evidence of the facts of the Resurrection as we would in a court of law, what will happen? Will the Resurrection be proved or disproved? In our next chapter, we will begin to examine the evidence to determine: Is the Resurrection a fact of history or merely a legend?

Two

EXAMINING THE EVIDENCE

Investigative Journalist Lee Strobel was once a critic of the Bible and a skeptic of the Resurrection. Through a series of circumstances, he began an all-out investigation of the truth of Christianity. He writes:

> Setting aside my self-interest and prejudices as best I could, I read books, interviewed experts, asked questions, analyzed history, explored archaeology, studied ancient literature, and for the first time in my life picked apart the Bible verse by verse.
>
> I plunged into the case with more vigor than with any story I had ever pursued. I applied the training I had received at Yale Law School as well as my experience as legal affairs editor of the *Chicago Tribune*. And over time the evidence of the world—of history, of science, of philosophy, of

psychology—began to point toward the unthinkable.[1]

Eventually, the evidence of the life of Jesus and his Resurrection so changed Lee Strobel's life that today he is a Christian speaker, author, and filmmaker living in Southern California!

What evidence did Lee Strobel and other investigators discover in their search for the truth of the Resurrection?

1. The Empty Tomb

Gary R. Habermas, PhD confidently says, "The Resurrection is the cornerstone of our [Christian] faith."[2] And the most important fact of the Resurrection is that the tomb was empty of the body. How do we know this for sure?

The Jewish leaders who despised Jesus had heard his prophesy that he was going to come back again. Therefore, they wanted to ensure that his disciples didn't steal the body to pretend that the prophecy came true and went to Pilate with a request that he secure the tomb of Jesus. In response to their request, Pilate installed a Roman guard of 16 men in front of the tomb and sealed the tomb with a two-ton stone with his own seal on the stone (Matt. 27:62-66) in response to their request. Surely a weak band of followers like the disciples wouldn't be able to get past a trained Roman guard. Yet in spite of the soldiers' best efforts, they couldn't keep Jesus in the tomb. On the third day, he walked right out of the grave.

Just imagine how the religious leaders took the news of the Resurrection! An interesting story is told in Matthew about the Jewish priests' reaction to the news that Jesus had risen from the dead. The tomb guards were concerned about their own welfare because they had failed in their mission and could be punished by execution, perhaps even Crucifixion. Some of the guards came and told the priests what had happened at the tomb. The priests bribed the guards to spread the story that the disciples stole the body (Matt. 28:11-15). These were the actions of a desperate group who were afraid of Jesus!

Apologetics author Ralph Muncaster, former skeptic, writes:

> It would have been virtually impossible for the misfit band of disciples to overcome the guard and steal the body of Jesus. Nor would they have any reason to do so.

Despite the explanation presented by the Jewish leaders and the Roman guards that the disciples had stolen the body, the city of Jerusalem was not accepting it. Instead, the people accepted the story presented by the eyewitnesses that Jesus had rose from the dead. Many gave their lives to verify this strong belief.

In a nutshell, all the Jewish leaders and Romans had to do in order to end Christianity forever was to produce the corpse of Jesus. They couldn't do it. And Christianity has since become the largest religion in the world. *The tomb was empty.*[3]

2. The Lives of the Disciples

Among the most convincing proofs of the reality of Jesus' Resurrection was the change in the lives of the disciples. They changed from being scared and scattered followers to being confident and courageous evangelists who did not fear for their lives. In fact, all of them but one died gruesome deaths as martyrs because of their testimony that Christ rose from the dead.

Peter, the disciple who denied Jesus during his trial just before his execution, clearly attests, "For we were not making up clever stories when we told you about the power of our Lord Jesus Christ and his coming again. We have seen his majestic *splendor* [emphasis added] with our own eyes" (2 Pet. 1:16, NLT). What *splendor* was Peter talking about? The resurrected Christ!

Who were these disciples? Were they extraordinary people who were prepared from childhood to represent Jesus? Jerry Rose, former president of the National Religious Broadcasters, says, "As individuals, they were completely unremarkable, middle class at best. They came from all walks of life—fishermen, a tax collector, even a militant rebel. But drawn together by the Messiah himself, this unlikely band of brothers would change the world."[4]

After Christ's Crucifixion, this band of followers scattered, cowering behind locked doors, in fear for their own lives. What changed them? A miracle beyond what they could ever dream—the Resurrection of Jesus Christ. From those early days on, they became a powerful force that spread the news of this miraculous event that changed the world in one generation.

But no one was in the tomb during the Resurrection. How could the disciples be sure that it actually happened? Because Jesus physically appeared to them numerous times after the Resurrection. John tells of the first appearance in his Gospel:

> On the evening of that first day of the week, when the disciples were together, with the doors locked for fear of the Jews, Jesus came and stood among them and said, "Peace be with you!" After he said this, he showed them his hands and side. The disciples were overjoyed when they saw the Lord (John 20:19-20, NIV).

But one disciple was not present— Thomas. When he heard of the experience the other disciples had with Jesus, he doubted that it was true. We can feel sympathetic toward Thomas. He was filled with grief; he thought he would never see Jesus again. All his hopes for the future had been dashed. Although Thomas has the reputation as the doubting disciple, none of Jesus' followers believed in the Resurrection until they saw the proof for themselves—his presence among them.

The apostle John writes about what happened when Jesus appeared to Thomas:

Now Thomas (called Didymus), one of the Twelve, was not with the disciples when

Jesus came. So the other disciples told him, "We have seen the Lord!"

But he said to them, "Unless I see the nail marks in his hands and put my finger where the nails were, and put my hand into his side, I will not believe it."

A week later his disciples were in the house again, and Thomas was with them. Though the doors were locked, Jesus came and stood among them and said, "Peace be with you!" Then he said to Thomas, "Put your finger here; see my hands. Reach out your hand and put it into my side. Stop doubting and believe."

Thomas said to him, "My Lord and my God!" (John 20:24-28, NIV).

One of the most amazing facts of the transformation of the disciples is that they had no reason to claim that Jesus had been raised from the dead. When jurors sit on a case in a court trial, one of the questions they ask about the testimony of the witnesses is: "What does this person have to gain by giving this testimony?" For some, it could be that the testimony will lead to financial gain or status. That puts their testimony into question.

But the disciples had nothing to gain by attesting to the Resurrection—not wealth, political gain or prestige. They weren't going to get a retirement fund set up in their names or a villa at a Roman resort. The apostles received no benefits outside their reward in the eternity. In fact, they were persecuted and executed for their faith. But they were so convinced that Jesus rose from the dead and was alive that they endured beatings, stoning, ridicule, loss of family, and horrific deaths. There is no doubt that they valiantly claimed to have seen him alive with their own eyes.

3. The Historical Record

The main written record of the Resurrection is contained in the four Gospels of the New Testament (Matthew, Mark, Luke, and John). Most accounts are found in Matthew 28, Mark 16, Luke 24, and John 20, 21. In Acts 2, the apostle Peter preaches a sermon to a gathered crowd of thousands in which he attests to the Resurrection of Jesus.

Later, the apostle Paul, who began as one of the religious leaders who persecuted Christians before his conversion, gave his testimony to the truth of the Resurrection. He writes:

For what I received I passed on to you as of first importance: that Christ died for our sins according to the Scriptures, that he was buried, that he was raised on the third day according to the Scriptures, and that he appeared to Peter, and then to the Twelve. After that, he appeared to more than five hundred of the brothers at the same time, most of whom are still living, though some have fallen asleep. Then he appeared to James, then to all the apostles, and last of all he appeared to me also, as to one abnormally born (1 Corinthians 15:3-8, NIV).

But what about secular sources? Can we find any proof of the Resurrection of Jesus in sources other than the Bible?

Beyond the Bible, there are more than 20 non-Christian sources written between 30 and 130 AD that refer to Jesus of Nazareth as a historical figure. Twelve mention his death and provide details on how he died. Ten of these refer to his Resurrection.

Thallus, a Samaritan historian, who wrote around 52 AD, explained the darkness that occurred during the Crucifixion as a solar eclipse. According to modern astronomy, there was no eclipse at that time, but Scripture tells us "from the sixth hour until the ninth hour, darkness came over all the land" (Matt. 27:45, NIV). Thallus's account was referenced by Julius Africanus.[5]

The Jewish historian Josephus, who lived in the second half of the first century, wrote that the disciples believed that Jesus had risen from the dead:

> And there was about this time Jesus, a wise man if indeed one ought to call him a man. For he was the achiever of extraordinary deeds and was a teacher of those who accept the truth gladly. He won over many Jews and many of the Greeks. He was the Messiah. When he was indicted by the principal men among us and Pilate condemned him to be Crucified, those who had come to love him originally did not cease to do so; for he appeared to them on the third day restored to life, as the prophets of the Deity had foretold these and countless other marvelous things about him. And the tribe of Christians, so named from him, has not disappeared to this day (Antiquities 18:63-64).[6]

Another historian during that time period was Cornelius Tacitus, (55 AD–117 AD), a Roman historian. He writes, "Christus, from whom the name [Christians] had its origin, suffered the extreme penalty during the reign of Tiberius at the hands of one of our procurators, Pontius Pilate, and a most mischievous superstition ... broke out not only in Judea, the first source of the evil, but even in Rome ..."[7]

The "mischievous superstition" most likely referred to the spread of the news of the Resurrection. The spread of the Resurrection account throughout the known world spawned the growing movement of a new sect: "Christians." Their willingness to risk persecution and join the unpopular movement of Believers demonstrated that the Early Christians believed the first-hand reports of eyewitnesses of the resurrected Jesus still living at that time.

To counter the skeptics that say the Resurrection was a legend, Dr. William Lane Craig, Christian philosopher and theologian, says "the short time span between Christ's Crucifixion and the composition of this early Christian creed [of the death and Resurrection of Christ] precludes the possibility of legendary corruption."[8]

Taken together, the historical sources that mention Jesus and the Resurrection provide substantive evidence that the event was real. This amount of written testimony for any event in history in those early days is almost impossible to find. Yet, the Resurrection of Jesus has multiple sources of documentation. Cumulatively, these accounts add authenticity that the Resurrection is a factual historical event rather than a legend fabricated and passed down over time.

4. Jesus Didn't Die on the Cross

One of the most prevalent skepticisms about the Crucifixion and the Resurrection was that Jesus didn't really die on the cross but fainted or swooned and was revived in the coolness of the tomb. In other words, Jesus wasn't resurrected because he didn't really die.

Modern medical science has now refuted the claim, that Jesus could have survived the cross and preceding beatings resulting in massive blood loss.

What is so significant about this account? Alexander Metherell, MD, PhD, University of California at Irvine, is a medical doctor proficient in medical diagnoses. He asserts that the flogging Jesus received with a Roman *flagrum* was a significant factor in his death.

The Roman *flagrum,* an instrument of torture, was a whip that had pieces of metal or bone attached to the ends of the lashes. In some cases, a flogging with a *flagrum* alone was enough to cause death. The metal-studded whip dug into the skin and muscles of the victim and pulled out pieces of flesh until they were shredded and quivering. The flogging induced heavy blood loss. As was seen depicted in the Crucifixion story, Jesus was already suffering heavily as he walked to Golgotha. On the way to Calvary, he was unable to carry his cross, so the Roman guards forced a bystander to carry it for him. At this time, says Dr. Metherell, Jesus was already in serious to critical condition medically.[9]

One symptom of the massive loss of blood from flogging was that the victim became very thirsty, a condition of hypovolemic shock. John 19:28 tells of how Jesus cried out from the cross that he was thirsty, and the soldiers lifted up a sponge soaked in wine vinegar to his lips.

Victims of Crucifixion normally died of asphyxiation. As they were hanging, arms extended, wrists nailed, from the crossbeam, they had to strenuously push themselves up by their feet nailed to a crossbeam in order to exhale. In time, they became too fatigued to push themselves up and could no longer breathe.

Since Sabbath began at sundown and the Jewish leaders didn't want to leave the bodies on the cross during the Sabbath, the soldiers broke the legs of the Crucified thieves on either side of Jesus to cause them to asphyxiate quickly. But when they came to Jesus, he was already dead.

The only disciple brave enough to watch the execution of Jesus was John. He gives an eyewitness account of what happened to Jesus on the cross:

> One of the soldiers, however, pierced his side with a spear, and blood and water flowed out. This report is from an eyewitness giving an accurate account; it is presented so that you also can believe (John 19:34–35, NLT).

This outflow of blood and water was most likely because Jesus died of congestive heart failure secondary to asphyxia, according to Dr. Metherell.

> When the spear penetrated Jesus' side, it probably went through the lung and into the heart. When the spear was pulled out,

blood flowed out and then the clear fluid that had gathered around the heart, which would have looked like water. What John wrote in the Bible is consistent with medical fact.[10]

The blood stains on the Shroud bear further proof that "blood and water" flowed out of Jesus' side.

5. Eyewitnesses

We have already seen that the disciples were eyewitnesses that Jesus had raised from the dead. He appeared to them on numerous occasions over a period of time. Acts 1:3 (NIV) records:

> After his suffering, he showed himself to these men and gave many convincing proofs that he was alive. He appeared to them over a period of forty days and spoke about the Kingdom of God.

From these accounts we can clearly see that Jesus himself wanted to convince them that he was truly alive. But they were not the only ones to see Jesus. The Bible records that on one occasion, more than 500 people saw him at one time (1 Corinthians 15:6).

Here are some of the other people who were eyewitnesses to Jesus' return:

Mary Magdalene . . . . John 20:10-18

The other women at
the tomb . . . . Matthew 28:8-10

Simon Peter in Jerusalem . . . . . . Luke 24:34

The two travelers on
the road . . . . Mark 16:12,13

Ten disciples behind
closed doors . . . . John 20:19-25

All the disciples, with Thomas
(excluding Judas Iscariot) . . John 20:26-31

Seven disciples while
fishing . . . . John 21:1-14

Eleven disciples on
the mountain . . . . Matthew 28:16-20

Jesus' brother James, the apostles
and Paul . . . . 1 Corinthians 15:7

Those who watched Jesus ascend
into heaven ....Acts 1:3-8

During these appearances, Jesus let people touch him. He ate with them. He traveled with his friends and explained the Scriptures to them, especially how the Old Testament predicted his death and Resurrection. And he continued teaching with his emphasis on "the Kingdom of Heaven."

Some of his followers even saw him ascend into heaven when his work on Earth was completed. In all cases, the ones who witnessed his appearances were convinced beyond doubt that he was the same person who died on the cross just a few days earlier. Having eyewitnesses would be critical in their testimony as Jewish Law requires the testimony of at least two or three witnesses in a court of law.

6. The Change in the apostle Paul

One of the most telling examples of a person who saw Christ and whose life was transformed was the apostle Paul. He had been educated with the finest Jewish education, and he had a reputation as a well-trained and respected religious leader. Because of his position and his belief that Jesus and his disciples' claims were false, he hated the new sect of Christian believers. In fact, he was present at the stoning of the first Christian martyr, Stephen (See Acts 6, 7). Before his conversion, Paul was called Saul.

After a personal encounter with the Resurrected Christ who spoke to him (Acts 9), Paul realized that he had been fighting against the very One who had validated his universal authority through the Resurrection. The day that he met Jesus on the road to Damascus, Paul's focus in life changed 180 degrees from the persecution of the budding Christian faith to becoming its foremost proponent and evangelist to the corners of the Roman Empire. Now Paul was fully convinced that the Resurrection was a true fact of history.

Paul's reputation as a persecutor of the Church was so widespread that initially the Christians were afraid to accept him into their group. Eventually, Paul was imprisoned in Rome and martyred because he would not back down from proclaiming the message of the Crucified and Resurrected Christ. Paul was so convinced that the Resurrection of

Jesus from death unto life that he claimed the entire Christian faith rested on this one central truth of the Resurrection and its implications for all believers:

> And if Christ has not been raised, our preaching is useless and so is your faith. More than that, we are then found to be false witnesses about God, for we have testified about God that he raised Christ from the dead …
>
> And if Christ has not been raised, your faith is futile; you are still in your sins. Then those also who have fallen asleep [died] in Christ are lost. If only for this life we have hope in Christ, we are to be pitied more than all men.
>
> But Christ has indeed been raised from the dead, the first fruits [the first to be raised to life] of those who have fallen asleep [died] (1 Corinthians 15:14-15, 17-20, NIV).

The Church rapidly grew from a small band of disciples to a worldwide movement. Thousands of early believers were martyred for their faith in the first few centuries of Christianity. The Resurrection is truly one of the most attested events in history.

Perhaps a single piece of evidence is not enough to convince a skeptic that the Resurrection is true. But a court of law recognizes something called the "preponderance of evidence." This means that evidence builds, making the case stronger and stronger. The chapters that follow will enable us to examine the variety of historical, archaeological, medical and scientific evidences as we build *The Case for Christ's Resurrection.*

Endnotes

1   Lee Strobel, *The Case for Christ: A Journalist's personal Investigation of the Evidence for Jesus* (Grand Rapids, MI: Zondervan Publishing House, 1998), P. 14.

2   Gary R. Habermas, *The Case for Christ's Resurrection,* DVD, David W. Balsiger, senior producer, Grizzly Adams Productions, Inc., 2007.

3   Ralph O. Muncaster, *Examine the Evidence* (Eugene, OR: Harvest House Publishers, 2004), P. 393.

4   *Twelve Ordinary Men,* DVD, David W. Balsiger, senior producer, Grizzly Adams Productions, Inc., 2005.

5   Ralph O. Muncaster, *What Is the Proof for the Resurrection?* (Eugene, OR: Harvest House Publishers, 2000), P. 16.

6   Ibid. 13

7   Gary R. Habermas and Michael R. Licona, *The Case for the Resurrection of Jesus* (Grand Rapids, MI: Kregel Publications, 2004), P. 44, 45.

8   Dr. William Lane Craig, *Reasonable Faith,* 285, as cited by Hank Hanegraff, *Resurrection* (Nashville, TN: Word Publishing, 2000), P. 39.

9   *The Case for Christ's Resurrection,* DVD

10   Ibid.

THREE

A GHOSTLY IMAGE

Except for the faint images on the cloth of what looks like a crucified man, the cloth is unremarkable. Yet it is without doubt the most picked at, probed, X-rayed, examined, revered, reviled, tested, studied, scanned, and photographed object in the world today. That is no small thing when you consider that the Shroud has only been displayed in public fewer than twenty times in the last six-hundred years.

For centuries, few even knew of its existence as a complete Shroud, but over the years a growing number of people have become aware of the artifact, and many of them accept it as authentic on faith alone. With an increasing number of adherents, has come a growing body of scholarly opinion, most favoring authenticity. But a small group, bolstered by a 1988 Carbon-14 test, insists this cloth is nothing more than an elaborate medieval fraud.

The mystery of the Shroud of Turin is unquestionably the most sensitive, controversial, and emotional enigma in the world today. It may also be the most bitterly disputed, precisely because the positions taken on both sides are powerfully and persuasively presented.

Discovering whether the image on the Shroud is fact or fable is the purpose of this book. The questions are easily stated: Is the Shroud of Turin the burial cloth that covered Jesus Christ when his crucified body was laid in the tomb? Or is it a clever and elaborate medieval fraud?

The answers have been close to impossible to come by ... until now.

Over the past half century, the Shroud of Turin has brought together a strange assortment of "bedfellows." Scientists, researchers, skeptics, and believers are all seeking the true, scientific, and spiritual explanation for the hauntingly beautiful image on this patched and scorched ancient fabric. But an explanation that everyone can agree upon has eluded even the most ardent investigators.

The modern controversy began in 1898 when a gifted Italian photographer, Secondo Pia, was given unprecedented permission by the King of Italy to photograph the Shroud. It was exposed for eight days in commemoration of the 50th anniversary of the Kingdom of Italy.

* * *

"Hurry," Secondo said to his assistant, "we must hurry or we'll lose the light." Secondo Pia had spent the past week in preparation for this singular event. The king and the clerics had finally agreed to let him photograph the Shroud, and he knew he only had a precious few minutes when the light streaming in from the windows would be sufficient to let him capture the image on the glass plates in his camera. He had studied the great hall where the Shroud was now hanging, precisely where he had told the clerics to hang it to take full advantage of the afternoon sunlight. The clerics who guarded the cloth had grumbled at having to remove the ornate silver casket from behind the triple-locked iron gates beneath the nave of the cathedral, but in the end, facing an edict from both the

Cardinal and the king, they obeyed. But Pia knew that if he failed to capture the Shroud image on his fragile glass plates, he was not likely to get another opportunity.

With a photographer's precision, he had measured the distance from where the Shroud would hang to the platform upon which he and his camera would stand. Like most Italians, Pia had never seen the Shroud, but had only heard of it. He knew its length and width and color, but it was the ghostly image of the Christ supposedly imprinted on the cloth that had excited his imagination as a photographer. Just to see the Shroud in one's lifetime was a stroke of good fortune. Even the clerics who kept watch over it might have never seen it. Public exhibitions of the Shroud were typically many, many years apart, and so far as anyone knew, it was never unrolled in between those infrequent showings. That was, he remembered with a smile, the very argument that had convinced the king that the Shroud should be photographed. The Cardinal, on the other hand, was swayed more by the suggestion that the image might be fading.

"What if it disappears altogether?" Pia had pleaded, "and the next time you show it, there is nothing there?"

That fear and a secret desire on the part of the Cardinal to actually see the image may have been what prompted him to perpetuate the Shroud forever in a photograph.

The Photograph Is Taken

Secondo entered the great hall just as the clerics finished hanging the Shroud in its place. Silk ribbons were used to secure it to the beam, and no one but the priests and a select group of nuns who had given their lives to the protection of the Shroud were allowed to touch it. The king and the cardinal were present with a handful of soldiers who had accompanied the king to the cathedral. Shortly, the public would be allowed into the hall for a few precious moments. But now, hidden under the cape that covered his viewfinder, Pia would be alone with the Shroud.

Pia looked up in breathless anticipation, then his heart sank. From where he stood, the image looked more like faint smudges on the cloth, barely visible to the eyes. He quickly mounted the platform and began setting up the camera. With "last chance" foresight, he had ordered wheels put underneath the platform so that he could easily move closer and even take the photographs from a different angle if needed.

As soon as the camera was assembled, Secondo ducked under the cape that protected the viewfinder and began giving instructions to his assistant. "Closer ... and more to the right ... That's it ... That's it ... Stop!"

A few more seconds, and Secondo Pia popped out from under the cape and removed the cover on the lens. With intense attention to every detail, he counted the seconds, then quickly replaced the cap. This scenario was repeated several more times until Pia was satisfied that he had captured the Shroud in every possible light angle available to him. Still unsure of what his day's work might produce, he pronounced the job done and began dismantling his equipment, taking special care with the precious glass plates.

Back in his studio, Pia began processing the plates. His expectations were not high. After all, he had barely been able to make out the image in his viewer. Then, at that moment in the chemical bath, the image began to take shape. He gasped, staring in disbelief as he lifted the photograph from the chemical bath. It couldn't be …

* * *

In fact, what Pia caught on his photographic plates stunned the world. The faint, almost ghostlike images on the Shroud appeared in reverse on his camera plate, making it a positive image. It was the first time in history the likeness could be seen in full, majestic detail. When the photographs were released to the public, those who believed the Shroud was the burial cloth of Jesus could only stare in breathless wonder at the starkly beautiful image. There, in overwhelming detail, were the marks of the cruel crown of thorns, the bloody imprint of the nails, even the unmistakable scars of the vicious Roman *flagrum*.

The word spread like wildfire throughout the Christian world. The photographs seemed to prove what had only been an assumption: This was the burial Shroud of Christ.

Or was it?

Instant Controversy

The cries of the critics were instantaneous, loud, and persistent. "It's a fraud!" "A painting!" One critic even credited it to the work of Michelangelo, another to Leonardo DaVinci. Secondo Pia's amazing photograph had introduced a whole new level of controversy into the subject of, not just the Shroud, but the Resurrection itself. And if it was a painting, as some suggested, Pia's photograph had also introduced a new anonymous artist of amazing skill and artistry.

Or was it possible that his amazing photograph revealed nothing less than a tangible record of the Resurrection of Jesus Christ? The controversy swirled.

The Pros and Cons

This obscure artifact, tucked away in what was once the place of private worship of the Dukes of Savoy, eventual rulers of Italy, went largely unnoticed by the world for centuries. Now the stark reality of the photograph was there for all to see.

The controversy set up battle lines between those who believed the cloth was sacred and those who said it was fake. Each side had compelling arguments. And neither side would budge.

Pro: Reverent Care of the Shroud

To describe the Shroud as "tucked away" is not an exaggeration. The *Sancta Sindone*, or "Holy Shroud," as it is known to the Italians, was kept in the Turin Cathedral of St. John the Baptist. To reach it, a visitor was required to traverse the length of the cathedral and go up a flight of stairs by the side of the main altar. There one entered a baroque chamber lined with white marble tombs and a soaring cupola known as the Guarini chapel, the private chapel of the Italian royal family, the Savoys. In the center of this chapel was an ornate black marble altar set on a stepped platform. This altar was surmounted by a second altar, and it was here, in a locked space behind iron grilles for centuries, that the Shroud was kept for safety. The Shroud linen was rolled around a velvet spool and then wrapped in red silk and placed within a four-foot-long jewel-encrusted silver reliquary on which were the emblems of the Passion.

Probably no artifact in history has been the subject of more reverent care. The casket is kept within an iron chest wrapped in asbestos and sealed by no fewer than three locks, for each of which a separate key is required.[1] This care has been constant since the Middle Ages.

Why would so much attention be given to a fraud? Who would take this much time to preserve something of doubtful value? Duke Louis I of Savoy traded two castles to Margaret de Charny in 1453 to obtain possession of the Shroud. He was contemporarily in a position to know if the Shroud was a painted fake. He obviously knew and believed it was not.

Con: Just a Painting

Is it possible that for centuries all of this love and devotion had been lavished on nothing more than a clever painting? Dr. Walter McCrone, a chemical microscopist, insisted that is exactly what happened. "It is an absolute fact that the Shroud is a painting, period. When I started working on it, I expected it to be real. I was hoping it would be real. I can't argue, however, with the microscope."[2]

Except for the scientists who conducted Carbon-14 tests on a piece of fabric taken from the Shroud, Dr. McCrone stands virtually alone in his insistence that the Shroud is a painting. But if it is a painting, then the truth needs to be published so that people are not deluded any longer.

Pro: The "Painting" Is Anonymous

As Pia's photograph revealed, the Shroud contains an almost imperceptible image of amazing detail. If this image is a painting, we have a remarkably gifted artist who prefers to remain perhaps the most famous "ghost" in the history of art, a circumstance that seems totally out of character for any artist in any age. And, as we will see later, if the image is the work of some anonymous painter, he was an artist who needed to have much more information than was available during medieval times. These two facts strengthen the case that this is an actual artifact, not a painting, plus the fact that the image does not permeate the fibrils of the cloth but is only on the top of the fibrils—only a few microns in depth. Yet the blood stains on the image do permeate the fibers, as would be expected of genuine blood.

Con: Lack of Chain of Custody

As with any piece of evidence, the chain of custody is an essential element. That's why police detectives seal crucial evidence in a container and sign for it. Each time it is passed into someone else's hands, a record is made so that no one can doubt the evidence's validity. If the court doesn't know where the evidence has been, its authenticity and validity can be questioned.

If historians cannot account for location and custody of the Shroud through the hundreds of years of its claimed existence, then its history is in doubt. As we will see later, from around 1350 AD to the present, the whereabouts of the Shroud is documented. Before that, its history becomes less certain.

Pro: Science vs. Science

Ian Wilson has introduced one of the most interesting aspects of the ongoing debate—science versus science. "Whatever else it may be, the Shroud of Turin is most definitely not a fraud," he writes. "Many of today's most distinguished scientists, from dozens of different specialties and scientific fields, are convinced that the Shroud is genuine. These scientists not only believe in its authenticity, but also believe that the weight of scientific proof supports their belief."[3]

How could so many specialists, working independently in most cases and together in others, come to the same conclusion—that the Shroud leads us back to the Resurrection of Christ? Can they all be wrong?

Con: The D'Arcis Memorandum

Is there any way to shed enough light on the subject to give substance to this ethereal image? There is, after all, a great deal at stake. If the Shroud is a fake, it is arguably the most astonishing fake of all time. If it is genuine, then it is tangible proof of the Resurrection. There is no middle ground. It is one or the other.

Since it would appear to be of transcendent importance to Christians generally and specifically to the Catholic Church, what is the view of the Church? Surprisingly, the Church has remained silent regarding the matter of authenticity. A statement from a Catholic Bishop written in the form of a letter to the Pope is perhaps the most critical condemnation of the Shroud as an authentic artifact.

The now famous "Scandal at Lirey" letter or "D'Arcis Memorandum" was written in 1389 by Bishop D'Arcis, who lived in medieval France. The letter states that the image on the Shroud is a fake. The Bishop claims that abuses were perpetrated, "… so that from all parts people came to view it, and further to attract the multitude so that money might cunningly be wrung from them, pretended miracles were worked, certain men being hired to represent themselves as healed at the moment of the exhibition of the Shroud, which all believed to be the Shroud of our Lord."[4]

It would seem that something as clear as the D'Arcis Memorandum would have ended the matter once and for all. Unfortunately, the letter simply added another level to the controversy. We will go into more detail about the letter later.

Pro: D'Arcis Memorandum Isn't Authentic

But some researchers question the authenticity of the D'Arcis Memorandum rather than the authenticity of the Shroud. In the same publication from which this translation of the letter was published, the editor states flatly, "No fair copy of this document and no record of its having been sent [to the Vatican] is to be found in the official archives of the Chancellery."[5]

Ian Wilson echoes that sentiment:

The reputed Bishop D'Arcis letter has never been proved genuine. It is, in fact, somewhat questionable in itself. The handwriting ... is definitely not that of Bishop D'Arcis, and there is also no proof that the Pope ever saw it, or that it was delivered to him. Neither has the slightest substantiating documentation ever been found to support these allegations. In addition, if the purported letter were actually written by Bishop D'Arcis, the allegations were things that he only heard of ... some thirty-four years later."[6]

It appears that the memorandum questioning the authenticity of the Shroud has its own problems with authenticity.

Con: Carbon-14 Dating

One of the biggest controversies in recent years is the finding of Carbon-14 testing that the Shroud of Turin is of medieval origin. When the results were published, they caused a firestorm of opinions. Some hailed the tests as the final step in proving the Shroud a fraud. Others questioned the methodology of the tests. Instead of bringing a solution to the question of the Shroud's authenticity, the testing deepened the battle lines.

With all the controversy swirling around the Shroud of Turin, the truth is almost impossible to discover. One moment it seems that the Shroud is a fake; the next moment, it seems genuine. It is essential then that we separate the facts from fiction in our search for the truth.

Endnotes

1   Ian Wilson, "The Shroud of Turin—Burial Cloth of Jesus Christ?" *Mysteries of the Ancient World.* (Banbury, CN: Dell Publishing, 1995), P. 9.

2   Walter McCrone, PhD, Interview, *The Shroud of Turin: Is It the Burial Cloth of Jesus?* DVD, David W. Balsiger, Senior Producer, Grizzly Adams Productions, Inc., 2000.

3   Wilson, 9.

4   De Nantes, Georges R.P., ed, "The Evidence of a Scientific Forger," *The Catholic CounterReformation in the XXth Century,* March 1991.

5   Ibid.

6   Ian Wilson, "The Shroud of Turin—Burial Cloth of Jesus Christ?" *Mysteries of the Ancient World* (Banbury, CN, Dell Publishing, 1995), P. 71.

FOUR

THE PROPERTIES OF A MYSTERY

In modern times, the Shroud of Turin has been examined under electron microscopes, studied through polarized light microscopes and fluoroscopes, and subjected to a wide variety of space-age technology, all in an effort to determine exactly what it is and how this mysterious image was formed. Yet, except for the image on the cloth, which is barely discernible to the naked eye, it can be easily defined with a simple tape measure and seamstress's practiced eye. Unlike the Holy Grail or the Ark of the Covenant or many other sacred icons that have been the subject of extensive searches by the faithful, the Shroud of Turin is a physical fact. It can be seen, touched, and yes, studied scientifically.

With Tape in Hand

The Shroud is a piece of fine linen cloth measuring 14 feet, 3 inches long and 3 feet, 7 inches wide. It is not a common type linen—but rather a Herringbone weave which was quite uncommon and would have been very costly. It includes a hand-sewn seam that was added at an unknown date. It is marred by full-length, dark lines, which are scorches from a fire that nearly destroyed it in 1532. Clearly visible patches cover the holes from that fire and diamond-shaped water stains mar the surface.

At one time, when Ian Wilson was invited to view the Shroud, he was permitted to touch the fabric. He says of that experience:

> The linen, though ivory-colored with age, was still surprisingly clean looking, even to the extent of a damask-like sheen. In the areas untouched by the ravages of history, it was in remarkably good condition. The texture was light and almost silky to the touch.
>
> The cloth is truly unique. Nowhere else does a grave cloth of any age or dimension even exist that exhibits the same characteristics—an indelible, full-length image of the front and back of the person who was buried in it. And the description is even more specific. On both the front and back of the man are what appears to be

marks of a vicious flogging from the neck to the calves of the legs. There are also markings that indicate the man had something with many sharp points pressed onto his head. The back view of the shoulders gives the definite impression that they were badly bruised, as one might expect if the man had been carrying something heavy shortly before his death. Deep wounds to the wrist and feet are easily identified as "puncture" wounds, and the visible distension of the thorax would seem to indicate death by asphyxiation.[1]

The Coins

Like any physical evidence at a trial, we can find clues to the Shroud's past through examining its surface. Can we find clues that suggest this particular piece of cloth is authentic and not a forgery, fake, or medieval hoax? What is needed is some sort of *signature* on the Shroud that indicates this could be the image of Jesus Christ. Some investigators believe there is such an identifying signature. In 1931, another Italian photographer, Giuseppe Enrie, was permitted to photograph the Shroud. The photographic technology he had at his disposal was far advanced from that of Secondo Pia. When subjected to high magnification, Enrie's photographs revealed that small coins had been placed over the eyes. This startling discovery was later confirmed and enhanced by the use of a space-age instrument called the VP-8 Image Analyzer. (This amazing device is discussed in greater detail in a later chapter.)

In an article published in the *Numismatist* in 1978, Dr. John Jackson, one of the first to see the image on the screen of the VP-8 Analyzer, wrote:

> The result of this process ... revealed objects resting on the eyes, objects which resembled small discs or buttons. In summary, the objects are circular, about the same size, and flat.[2]

Further research revealed these coins to be Roman leptons, or the traditional widow's mite of the Bible, the smallest coins minted at the time. One of these coins was minted by Pontius Pilate between 29 and 33 AD. It is the only coin ever minted with an astrologers staff and was never minted again by any official in Palestine or anywhere else, a fact that becomes extremely important in later scientific studies. This coin is on the anatomical right eye of the image and contains a rare misspelling that was unknown to numismatists until its discovery on the Shroud eye image in the late 20th century. This mistake and misspelling was subsequently confirmed when an actual Pilate lepton with the same misspelling found. The other coin, the imprint of which appears over the anatomical left eye of the image, is a Julia lepton, which was minted by Caesar in honor of his mother only in 29 AD.[3]

What does this discovery say about the argument that the image is a painting? Could the "clever" artist who created the image have been deft enough to paint these small coins? Nothing in the biblical record even hints at the tradition of putting coins on the eyes. But assuming for the moment that the artist was knowledgeable enough to know about it, was he also ingenious enough to paint these one-half inch coins with letters so small they can be seen only on good quality photographs? Wouldn't that have required the artist to have some photographic device that didn't exist in the 13th century? Many other scientific discoveries corroborate the evidence, such as the presence of specific pollens found on the Shroud, as well as myrrh and aloes and images of many plants and flowers whose common growing area is only in the region of Jerusalem, and which bloom only in the months of March and April.

The intriguing question is: How were the images imprinted on the cloth? According to Professor John L. Brown, an electron microscopist; "Some of the best scientists in the world have observed this [body] image, measured it, studied it, and still have no explanation for how the image was formed."[4]

Kevin Moran, an optical engineer, after examining the Shroud in considerable detail, has come to his own conclusions: "I feel," he says, "that the radiation that made the image was a direct result of the Resurrection."[5]

Although there are many theories as to how the image was made, it still cannot be reproduced by space age science and technology.

Two Cloths

The Scripture clearly describes the contents of the tomb—and it points to two cloths. Let's return to John 20:5-7 for verification:

[John] bent over and looked in at the strips of linen lying there but did not go in. Then Simon Peter, who was behind him, arrived and went into the tomb. He saw the strips of linen lying there, as well as the burial cloth that had been around Jesus' head. The cloth was folded up by itself, separate from the linen (NIV).

Mark Guscin, Coordinator of Historical Investigation, Centro Espanol de Sindonologia, tells us that the original Greek rendering of John's words is even more explicit:

The other disciple [John] ran more quickly than Peter and came first to the tomb and stooping, sees lying—the sheets. Comes therefore also Simon Peter following him and entered the tomb and he beholds the sheets lying, and the kerchief which was on the head of him, not with the sheets lying but apart, having been wrapped up in one place (John 20:5-7).[6]

"That is very unambiguous," Guscin continues. "There were two pieces of cloth in the tomb … the 'Sheets' and the 'Kerchief.' If it can be demonstrated that the Shroud of Turin is the 'sheet,' then the evidence strongly suggests the small piece of cloth in Oviedo is very likely the 'kerchief.'"[7]

Known as the "Sudarium of Oviedo," this piece of cloth has been housed in a cathedral in Oviedo, Spain, protected and venerated for hundreds of years and regarded by the faithful as the cloth spoken of by John as "folded up by itself, separate from the linen." But what was the purpose of the smaller cloth? Dr. Guscin explains:

> Part of the ancient Jewish burial custom was to cover the face of the dead, sparing the family further distress. The Sudarium, from the Latin, "face cloth," would have been placed over the head while Christ was still on the cross, and after the body was placed in the tomb and wrapped in the Shroud, the face cloth would be set aside.[8]

This is consistent with John's account where he states that the Sudarium was rolled up and in a place by itself. Dr. Guscin continues:

> It also explains why the Sudarium, although it has bloodstains, does not have any kind of image similar to that on the Shroud. If it were Christ's Resurrection that somehow transferred the image to the Shroud, that event would have taken place after the Sudarium had been removed and set aside. All of which sets the stage for

many other findings that seem to put the Sudarium and the Shroud of Turin in the same place at the same time.

The face cloth has been subjected to almost as much testing as the Shroud, and several important discoveries have been made. For example: the blood on both the Shroud and the Sudarium belongs to the same group—AB; the blood flow patterns on the Sudarium make it evident that the man whose face it covered was in an upright position; there are stains from deep puncture wounds on the portion of the Sudarium covering the back of the head consistent with those marks found on the Shroud of Turin; on both cloths there is a stain of identical shape, resembling the Greek Epsilon, appearing on the forehead; a separate set of stains was made when the crucified man was laid horizontally and lymph flowed from the nostrils.

The composition of the stain is one part blood and six parts pulmonary edema fluid. This liquid collects in the lungs when someone dies from asphyxiation, the real cause of death when a person is crucified; and the length of the nose through which the fluid came onto the Sudarium has been calculated at eight centimeters, exactly the same length as the nose on the image on the Shroud.[9]

The Preponderance of Evidence

What tends to give credence to Christian scholars is the extreme precision with which the Shroud reflects the description of the Passion of Christ as portrayed in the Bible. Of course, it can be argued that an expert in scriptural studies who was intent on proving the biblical story would know all those things and include them in his depiction. But that argument fails to explain the presence on the Shroud of things that are not part of the biblical account, like the coins on the eyes, the pollen, and the dim but distinct outline of hundreds of flowers, some of which have been identified as plants that grow only in and around Jerusalem.

We can then ask: Would a forger, knowing that every unnecessary brush stroke makes him more vulnerable to detection, take the risk of adding things to his work that are nowhere even alluded to in the biblical record? It doesn't seem very likely.

According to the gospels, "[*John*] *saw and believed.*" [John 20:8, NIV). What did he see that convinced him Jesus had been resurrected? Could it be that the Shroud and the Sudarium were lying undisturbed, just as they had been placed during the entombment? Is it possible that the image of their Lord on the Shroud was clearly visible to them? If that's true, imagine the dilemma faced by these two pious Jews who were also disciples of Jesus Christ. In the laws of Judaism, a burial cloth (or anything that touched a dead body) would have been considered "unclean," and it would have been considered unlawful for a Jew to touch anything unclean, and in this way become "defiled." It is doubtful then, that Peter and John as pious Jewish men of the first century, would have even considered touching the grave cloths they saw lying in the tomb ... unless there was something extraordinary about these burial linens that had once wrapped the body of Jesus.

We may never know exactly how the Shroud was removed from the tomb, but we can be fairly certain that it concerned the early church. Early church tradition says Peter took and kept the Shroud for a while. But the argument is less, "Who is the man in the Shroud?" than, "How did the image get there?" Theologians, skeptics, scientists, artists, and researchers from all disciplines seem to be *most* interested in seeking the answer to the simple question of how the image was imprinted on the cloth. After all, except for the image, the Shroud of Turin is simply a very long, very old piece of hand-woven linen cloth.

What the Shroud of Turin *is* then, is a piece of linen cloth bearing a faint image of a naked male corpse reflecting the marks of the Passion and Crucifixion that has been venerated for over two thousand years. It is a religious artifact of uncertain date and origin that has been accepted on faith by millions of Christians the world over as the genuine burial cloth of Jesus Christ.

Is it possible to separate fact from fiction? People on both sides of the controversy say "Yes!" Whether you believe the Shroud of Turin is a forgery or that it is authentic, a search for truth is desirable.

In the next few chapters, we will begin with the history of the Shroud and go on to science. We will search the answers to these questions:

1. Can we establish a timeline of the Shroud's history?

2. Is the Shroud a painting or other work of art?

3. What did the Carbon-14 testing reveal about the Shroud's age?

4. What do scientists of various disciplines say about the Shroud after examining it in recent years?

5. What hope does the Shroud give us for the authenticity of the cross and for the Resurrection?

6. Are new discoveries in quantum physics about the make-up of the universe relevant to the search for the truth about the Shroud?

The answers to these questions may take us to the beginning of creation itself!

Endnotes

1   Ian Wilson, Interview, *The Shroud of Turin: Is It the Burial Cloth of Jesus?* DVD, David W. Balsiger, Senior Producer, Grizzly Adams Productions, Inc., 2000.

2   Dr. John Jackson, *Numismatist,* 1978.

3   Michael Minor, Esq., A *Lawyer Argues for the Authenticity of the Shroud,* 1990.

4   John L. Brown, Interview, *The Shroud of Turin: Is It the Burial Cloth of Jesus*? DVD,

David W. Balsiger, Senior Producer, Grizzly Adams Productions, Inc., 2000.

5   Kevin Moran, Interview, *The Shroud of Turin: Is It the Burial Cloth of Jesus*? DVD, David W. Balsiger, Senior Producer, Grizzly Adams Productions, Inc., 2000.

6   Mark Guscin, Coordinator of Historical Investigation, Centro Espanol De Sindonologia, Interview, *The Fabric of Time*, DVD, David W. Balsiger, Senior Producer, Grizzly Adams Productions, Inc., 2006.

7   Ibid.

8   Ibid.

9   Ibid.

FIVE

THE HISTORY OF THE SHROUD

The modern history of the Shroud begins in a small wooden church in the provincial town of Lirey, France in the year 1357 AD. The Shroud's owner at the time, Geoffrey de Charny, had been killed by the English the year before at the Battle of Poitiers, and his widow, nearly destitute, sought to earn a little money by displaying the burial garment of the Savior in the Church of Lirey for whatever offerings the faithful might bring. The de Charnys didn't explain how an obscure French nobleman obtained possession of such a fabulous artifact. This is part of the mystery of the Shroud's whereabouts before the fourteenth century.

Skeptics argue that there is no historical trail tracing the Shroud's location prior to 1353 AD. That leaves a gap of some 1300 years from the time it was supposedly wrapped around Christ's body to the time it appeared in the church at Lirey, France.

Where was it all those years? Did it even exist during that period?

First Century Evidence

Some researchers believe that the Shroud not only existed, but its travels are well documented. Skeptics, these researchers say, are completely wrong in insisting that the trail to the Shroud only goes back to the mid-thirteen hundreds, and point out that it does go back to New Testament times.

The New Testament book of Luke, written by the first-century physician Luke in his attempt to document an accurate account of events, records how Joseph of Arimathea, a wealthy and powerful member of the Jewish Sanhedrin (the ruling council) who became a follower of Jesus, went to Pilate and asked for Jesus' body after he had died on the cross.

After taking the body down from the cross and wrapping it in a long linen cloth, he laid it in a new tomb carved out of rock. The women from Galilee who had been watching the Crucifixion events from a distance followed him to see where Jesus' body was being laid. Since it was already Friday evening and the beginning of the Sabbath, they had to wait until Sabbath was over to return to the tomb with the spices and ointments they had prepared for the body's burial.

Luke continues the account, describing how that early Sunday morning when the women—Mary Magdalene, Mary the Mother of Jesus, Salome and several other women arrived at the tomb, they discovered that the huge rolling stone that had covered the entrance had been rolled aside. And when they entered the tomb they were puzzled to find Jesus' body missing, so they hurried back to tell the eleven surviving disciples. The disciples reportedly did not believe their story, but Peter ran to the tomb and he entered the tomb to find the empty Shroud linens. He also left the tomb puzzling over what had happened. (Based on Luke 23:50–24:12.)

John 20:6 also describes Peter's entry into the tomb of Jesus on Sunday morning, when he found the Shroud. Normally, a grave cloth was considered unclean and destroyed, but this one bore the image of the Lord's body. That would explain why it may have been retrieved by Jesus' followers and treated with great reverence.

Further confirmation that this was the belief of the early church comes from a quotation from "The Life of St. Nino." On her deathbed in 338 AD, Saint Nino gave an account of what she had been taught in Jerusalem as a young girl:

> [T]hey found linen early in Christ's tomb, whither Pilate and his wife came ... Now they did not find the Shroud (Sudari), but it is said to have been *found by Peter who took it and kept it* [emphasis added], but we do not know if it has ever been discovered.[1]

Since historical researchers are generally reluctant to question the documented word of a saint giving her testimony on her deathbed, we can be fairly certain that early church followers were taught that Peter took possession of the burial cloth found in the empty tomb.

Two major documents help establish the link from the tomb to the second millennium: the Gregory Sermon of August 16, 944 AD, which strongly suggests that a full-length image on the cloth arrived from Edessa, and the Hungarian Pray Codex of 1192-5 AD. This codex shows Shroud-like folded hands without thumbs and a four burn-hole pattern that is still seen on the Turin Shroud.[2]

Fourth Century Portrayal

Some Shroud Scholars believe the Shroud was folded upon itself four times and placed inside a special coverlet or cloth envelope that had a round hole in the center of one side that allowed only the face to be seen. This envelope was then placed in a specially made container, or hung from a special frame with gold latticework. To protect it even further, the caretakers of the Shroud began to refer to it as the "Mandylion" (MAN-DILL'-EE-ON), a Greek term meaning simply "towel." The artifact was carefully guarded, and no one is sure just who had possession of it, but researchers point out that 300 years after the Crucifixion, something called the *Mandylion* was put on exhibition at Edessa in what is now Southern Turkey.[3]

However, around 30 AD, numerous references connected the Shroud with King Agbar in Turkey:

A 4th century Syriac manuscript records that the king of Edessa, a man named Abgar, was cured of leprosy when he received from a disciple a cloth that had upon it the image of Jesus' face.

In the year 30 AD, King Agbar V of Edessa, sent a message to Jesus asking him to come to Edessa and heal him of what probably was leprosy. Jesus sent the king a letter saying that his work was in Jerusalem, so he couldn't come, but he would send one of his helpers. (Some Eastern Orthodox churches claim to have copies of this letter.) Soon after, Jesus was crucified.

Dr. Alan and Mary Whanger write, "Eusebius (263-339 AD) reported in his history of the early church that an object, presumably a cloth with an image, was taken to King Abgar by one of Jesus' disciples in 30 AD and that King Agbar was healed."[4]

A 10th century icon in Saint Catherine's Monastery in the Sinai desert of Egypt shows Thaddeus (probably Judas the Zealot) bringing a cloth to King Agbar. On the cloth was an image and it was referred to as the *Mandylion*. King Agbar was healed and became a believer in Christ. He declared his city's allegiance to Jesus, and a church was established. The king destroyed the city's god and erected a tile bearing the face of the Mandylion over the city gate.

When King Agbar died, a pagan king came to power, and persecution against Christians broke out. To protect them, the tile and the cloth were hidden in a niche in the city wall. Later, the city of Edessa became mostly Christian. During repairs on the wall after a flood in 525 AD, the cloth was rediscovered. People instantly recognized it. Around 300 churches were built during this time, the largest being the Church of St. Addai which was built to house the *Mandylion.* The image became so widely known that most artistic works of Jesus resembled the image visible on the Shroud. Today, we would recognize those depictions as Jesus of Nazareth.[5]

According to Ian Wilson, the Church of St. Addai "was one of the most highly revered in Edessa because, as universally believed back in the first millennium, it had been Addai, as one of Jesus' seventy 'outer circle' of disciples, who had brought Christianity to Edessa only very shortly after Jesus' Crucifixion, healing Edessa's king of the time, Agbar, and converting him to Christianity."[6]

The Shroud evidently remained in Edessa until 944 AD when the Byzantine emperor sent an army to bring it to Constantinople.[7]

Byzantine records show that a great celebration and parade accompanied the Shroud's entry into Constantinople on August 15th, 944 AD where it was once again revered as the true and miraculous image of Christ. The Mandylion, or Shroud, apparently spent the next three centuries under the protection of Constantine and the subsequent kings of that Christian city, but then another army made history.

"Not Made by Human Hands"

According to Shroud historian Gian Maria Zaccone, "It is hard to follow development of the history of the image of Edessa which, for a period, disappears completely from descriptions of the city. It reappears in a chronicle of the Persian siege in 544 AD, written by Evagrius Scholasticus, some fifty years after the event. In this, the image of the Face is mentioned again, this time described as 'not made by human hands.' "[8]

Church Murals in the Catacombs

The uniformity of the images that portray Christ today appears to have its beginnings in the Byzantine era. Some earlier renditions of Christ's appearance, in certain places such as some of the Roman catacombs, apparently had been based on the Mandylion face, but many others were that of a young, beardless youth like the Greek god, Apollo. With the appearance of the Mandylion, the pictorial concept of Christ largely became the accepted version today—a mature man in his early thirties with a beard. Experts agree that what is known as the Mandylion of Edessa influenced the pictorial representations of Christ.

One of the greatest proofs for the authenticity of the Shroud is contained in the existence of the very early church murals found in the Roman catacombs or underground burial chambers. Those artists in no way could have seen the Shroud, yet the man in the paintings is identical to the man of the Shroud. These early representations of Christ in catacomb paintings were not created out of imagination, but the faithful depiction of someone who really existed. The paintings were done by eyewitnesses, or from the description of eyewitnesses, and is further proof that the Shroud is the imprint of the same man.[9]

Dr. Alan Whanger and his wife Mary have worked extensively with Byzantine paintings and other Byzantine-era icons to discover whether or not a valid, scientific comparison can be made to the Shroud. Their findings have added a whole new dimension to research efforts in dating, not just of the fabric, but of the image itself. In a taped interview, Dr. Whanger drew attention to specific icons:

> An early Coptic icon of Christ produced about 550 AD and presently located in St. Catherine's monastery at the base of Mt. Sinai is a highly accurate image derived from direct observation of the facial image on the Shroud of Turin. It has approximately 250 points of congruence with the Shroud image. In a court of law, it takes only 45 to 60 points of congruence to establish a positive identity of the same face. Such congruence points include a small tear from the left eye, chap marks on the lips, even the images of flowers around the head.
>
> The icon shows that the Shroud image was well-known at the time and [was] believed to be an authentic image and hence was used by the iconographers of the Byzantine period for their artistic productions from the 6th century on.[10]

Although the facts of the Shroud's early existence are cloaked in mystery, certain facts can be obtained from the historical record:

1) City records of Edessa in Southern Turkey show the arrival of the face image, (actually the Shroud folded so that only the facial image was exposed) in 30 AD.

2) Constantine VII sent an army from Constantinople to retrieve the Shroud (known as the "Image of Edessa") from Edessa.

3) Clerics risked their lives in the year 1532 to rescue it from a burning cathedral in Chambéry, France.

4) Certain medieval knights suffered death by fire rather than reveal its whereabouts.

5) For centuries it is believe to have been referred to simply as "The Mandylion," a Greek word meaning, "towel."

This summarizes the historically reliable record of the travels of the Shroud from the Crucifixion to the Middle Ages. Of course, that history maintains reliability only if it can be demonstrated that the Mandylion of Edessa is the same Shroud taken from the tomb of the crucified Christ. The attempt to answer that question follows in the next chapter.

Regardless of its history, one inescapable fact exists—a piece of linen cloth, believed by many to be the very piece of fabric used by Joseph of Arimathea as the burial Shroud for Jesus Christ, can be found today at the cathedral in Turin, Italy. It is known worldwide as the "Shroud of Turin," and if it is authentic, it is the most valuable antiquity of Christianity, and perhaps of any culture. The implications of this piece of linen cloth go far beyond any artifact ever known simply because it seeks to prove the Resurrection of Jesus Christ ... *if* ... it is authentic.

Endnotes

1   Albert Driesbach, Fr. "Did Peter See More Than an Empty Shroud?," Abstract, 1991.

2   Daniel Scavone, PhD, "Greek Epitaphoi and Other Evidence for the Shroud in Constantinople up to 1204," *Proceedings of the 1999 Shroud of Turin International Research Conference* (Richmond, Virginia, Magisterium Press, 2000), P. 196

3   Albert Driesbach, Fr. Interview, *Shroud of Turin: Is It the Burial Cloth of Jesus?* DVD. David W. Balsiger, Senior Producer, Grizzly Adams Productions, Inc., 2000.

4   Mary and Alan Whanger, *The Shroud of Turin: An Adventure in Discovery* (Franklin, TN: Providence House Publishers, 1998), P. 5.

5   Information taken from Whanger, *The Shroud of Turin*.

6   Ian Wilson, "Urfa Turkey, A Proposal for an Archaeological Survey of the Town That was the Shroud's Home for Nearly a Thousand Years," *Proceedings of the 1999 Shroud of Turin International Research Conference,* (Richmond Virginia, Magisterium Press, 2000), P. 221.

7   Albert Driesbach, Fr., *Shroud of Turin*.

8   Gian Maria Zacone, *On the Trail of the Shroud*, Alan Neame, trans. (Sydney, Australia: Daughters of St. Paul, 1998), P. 52, 53.

9   Taken from a lecture with slides, "From the Catacombs to the Present: The Arts Testify," by Isabel Piczek, unpublished notes.

10 Dr. Alan Whanger, *Shroud of Turin: Is It the Burial Cloth of Jesus?* DVD, David W. Balsiger, Senior Producer, Grizzly Adams Productions, Inc., 2000.

Six

THE MEDIEVAL CONNECTION

During the Crusades, in 1204 AD, European knights of the 4th Crusade stormed and sacked Constantinople. It is a well-known fact that Constantinople was eventually stripped of its treasury of art and relics. Two recently discovered documents show that the Shroud was carried to Athens, Greece in 1205 AD by a prominent knight of the 4th Crusade, Othon de la Roche. A French knight, Robert de Clari, wrote that he had seen the Shroud with the image of Christ on it, but that after the city fell, the Shroud mysteriously disappeared. For nearly 150 years, it vanished from the record. Where did it go? Surely a relic as famous and as revered as the Mandylion would be protected by all available means.

Many historians believe the Shroud was taken into safekeeping by the Knights Templar, then the most powerful organization in Europe. It is at this juncture that the final connection is made. A leading knight of the order at that time was Geoffrey de Charnay. It is believed the Shroud was obtained by him, and even though de Charnay was burned at the stake, he went to his grave without ever revealing its whereabouts.[1]

But why connect de Charnay to the Shroud? The records indicate that de Charnay was accused of idol worship because he venerated and would not recant his belief in the sacredness of some relic in his possession. If it is true that de Charnay was the knight who had possession of the Shroud, it may well have been the object of his veneration, and if it was, his devotion sealed his death. It is also interesting to note that none of the Knights Templar, if they knew about the Shroud, ever revealed the location of the Shroud, although many of them met the same fate as de Charnay.

Some years later, the undisputed historical chain of custody of the Shroud begins with another Geoffrey de Charny. The genealogy of both men is not clearly delineated, but since they both come from the same area of France, and since the names are virtually the same (only the letter "a" is missing from the younger de Charny's name), it is likely that the younger Geoffrey de Charny was a relative of the old knight. From this point on, the trail of the Shroud is very easy to follow and largely undisputed.

In about 1353 AD at Lirey, Jean de Vergie, a distant descendant of the aforementioned 13th century knight, Othon de la Rouche, married Geoffrey de Charny, the first documented owner of the Shroud. A pilgrim's medallion from about 1356 AD shows the family crest of Vergie and Charny side by side below the twin images of the Shroud, which suggests equal ownership between them.[2]

Geoffrey de Charny, when he endowed the collegiate church at Lirey, gave the Shroud into its keeping. Sixty years later, the de Charnys reclaimed the Shroud, and for another 34 years Margaret, de Charny's granddaughter, refused to return it to the church, even under the threat of excommunication. Finally, in 1452–53, Margaret transferred ownership of the Shroud to the Savoys, the royal family of Italy. In return, she received revenue from two castles, Miribel and Flummet.

Medieval Dissension

The medieval period in history also saw the rise of people who challenged the traditions of their faith. In 1389, Bishop D'Arcis, who lived in medieval France, penned the now famous "Scandal at Lirey" letter or "D'Arcis Memorandum." In this letter, he explained his views of the Shroud to his colleagues. In a missive that was purportedly written to the Pope, Bishop D'Arcis states:

> Diligent inquiry and examination by my predecessor, Bishop Henrie D'Potier, discovered out the fraud, that the false relic was nothing but a piece of common cloth, cunningly painted. Bishop D'Potier had a full confession from the culprit painter himself for which he immediately ordered withdrawal of the false relic from public view.[3]

Since the document is more or less central to the controversy, we have reproduced the translation that was published side by side with the original letter in the March 1991 issue of *The Catholic Counter Reformation in the XXth Century.* This entire issue was devoted to the Shroud of Turin. The D'Arcis Memorandum reads verbatim as follows:

Most Holy Father, some time since in the diocese of Troyes, the Dean of a certain collegiate church, that of Lirey, falsely and deceitfully, being consumed with the passion of avarice, and not from any motive of devotion but only of gain, procured for his church a certain cloth cunningly painted, upon which, by clever sleight of hand was depicted the twofold image of one man, that is to say, the back and front, he falsely declaring that and pretending that this was the actual Shroud in which your Savior Jesus Christ was enfolded in the tomb, and upon which the whole likeness of the Savior had remained thus impressed together with the wounds which he bore. This was put about not only in the kingdom of France, but, so to speak, throughout the whole world, so that from all parts people came to view it, and further to attract the multitude so that money might cunningly be wrung from them, pretended miracles were worked, certain men being hired to represent themselves as healed at the moment of the exhibition of the Shroud, which all believed to be the Shroud of our Lord. The Lord Henry of Pouters, of pious memory, then Bishop of Troyes, becoming aware of this, and urged by many prudent persons to take action as indeed was his duty in the exercise of his ordinary jurisdiction, set himself earnestly to work to fathom the truth of the matter. For many theologians and other wise persons declared that this could not be the real Shroud of our Lord having the Savior's likeness thus imprinted upon it, since the holy Gospel made no mention of any such imprint, while, if it had been true, it was quite unlikely that the holy Evangelists would have omitted to record it, or that the fact should have remained hidden until the present time. Eventually, after diligent enquiry and examination, he discovered the fraud and how the said cloth had been the object of artistic reproduction, as proved moreover by the artist who reproduced, (or depicted) it, and who attested it was the work of human skill and not miraculously wrought or bestowed. Accordingly, after taking mature counsel with wise theologians and men of the law, seeing that neither ought nor could allow the matter to pass, he began to institute formal proceedings against the said Dean and his accomplices in order to root out this false persuasion. They, seeing their wickedness discovered, hid away the said cloth so that the Ordinary could not find it, and they kept it hidden afterwards for thirty-four years or thereabouts down to the present year.[4]

D'Arcis's Arguments

D'Arcis claimed that not only was the cloth a fraud, but that the image had been painted for a purpose: to defraud the faithful and take their money. These were the times when Church hierarchy used indulgences, artifacts that they claimed would provide miracles if the penitent would pay some money and touch them. The Bishop then says that the cloth was exposed at the church in Lirey while the owners raked in the coins that the faithful gave.

Eventually, the Bishop of Troyes, who was alarmed about what was going on, set out to discover the truth about the Shroud and he claimed that he learned that the cloth was considered a fake. The letter further says that the Bishop of Troyes knew who had painted the image on the cloth. In fact, D'Arcis says that the artist who created the Shroud confessed to what he had done and as a result, the Bishop of Troyes "began to institute formal proceedings against the Dean of the Lirey church and his accomplices." For this reason, no one had seen the Shroud in 34 years.

The D'Arcis Memorandum was a harsh pronouncement, and if true, would negate any veneration of the Shroud. After all, as a fraud it was worthless. If it was created as a scam against the faithful, it was worthy only to be destroyed.

The Counterarguments

It would seem that something as clear and decisive as the D'Arcis Memorandum would have ended the battle over the authenticity of the Shroud once and for all. But it simply added another level to the controversy. The main thrust of the counterargument is that no one can say for sure that the letter itself is genuine.

In the same 1991 publication, *The Evidence of a Scientific Forger,* from which this translation of the D'Arcis Memorandum was taken, the editor states flatly, "No fair copy of this document and no record of its having been sent [to the Vatican] is to be found in the official archives of the Chancellery [or in the Vatican archives]."[5]

If this subject were so crucial at the time, why wasn't anything about the letter or information about the fraud ever recorded by the Church? Why did people continue to venerate it and why was the cloth protected and hidden?

Michael Minor, an attorney and author of *A Lawyer Argues for Authenticity of the Shroud of Turin*, goes on to explain:

> The reputed D'Arcis Memorandum has never been proved genuine. None of the copies of the D'Arcis Memorandum that we have are signed or dated; there's no proof that the Pope ever saw it or that it was ever delivered to him. And besides, no trace or hint of identity has ever been found of the artist, who if he ever made the image on the Shroud, would have belonged among the ranks of Michelangelo, DaVinci, and Raphael. The D'Arcis Memorandum lacks any probative value for several reasons ... but most convincing to me is the fact that it is neither signed nor dated; there is no evidence that it is in the handwriting of the Bishop that it's purported to be, and it is simply estimated that it is from about 1389. The artist or forger is not named, and there is no transcript of any sort of official investigation.[6]

The Theory Goes On

The D'Arcis Memorandum then appears to be little more than nebulous "hearsay" evidence. From reading the letter, it can't even be determined if Bishop D'Arcis had seen the Shroud himself.

But if the image was not "cunningly painted" in the Middle Ages, what else would tie the Shroud image to this period of history? And since the image unquestionably existed at that time period, those who support one or more of the various fraud theories, beginning with the Bishop D'Arcis Memorandum, are under some obligation to suggest methods by which the image was transferred onto the cloth.

The D'Arcis Memorandum highlights one of the most persistent arguments against the Shroud of Turin—that it is a medieval artist's conception of the Resurrection of Christ. That theory has gained ground over the years, and has some arguments in support of it. In the next chapter, the views of one of the most famous proponents of the "painting" theory, Dr. Walter McCrone, will be examined.

The Fire that Damaged the Shroud

On December 4, 1532, a fire in the Sainte Chapelle in Chambéry, France, (the Savoy Cathedral), damaged the Shroud.

How was it miraculously rescued from the flames? According to attorney, author, and

Shroud researcher, Michael Minor: "There was no time to find the custodians of the keys to unlock the Shroud from its iron-grilled repository. The Shroud was rescued on that occasion through the heroic efforts of a local blacksmith, but not before it sustained the most serious damage ever done to it. The heat from the Chambéry fire was so intense that molten globules of silver from the reliquary containing the Shroud dropped through one corner of the multi-folded Shroud causing burn holes along both edges. Miraculously, the image on the Shroud was virtually unscathed."[7]

Even previous to the Savoys establishing their capital in the city of Turin, they took the Shroud to Turin to be venerated by Cardinal Charles Borromeo, now "Saint Charles Borromeo."[8] The Shroud remains in Turin to this day. Apparently, the Savoys were not interested in earning worldly acclaim for their marvelous possession because after 1580, the Shroud was rarely exhibited to the public—only some 11 times in 400 years.[9] Probably as a result of the fire and fearing that too much exposure could further damage the cloth, clerics rarely permitted its showing in public.[10]

Recapping the Medieval History

We are indebted to Ian Wilson for his meticulous research on the Shroud's history during the Middle Ages beginning in 1349. We have included a brief excerpt from his chronicle of the undisputed history of the Shroud:

APRIL 1349: The Hundred Years War had been raging between France and England for over eleven years ... when Geoffrey de Charny wrote to Pope Clement VI reporting his intention to build a church at Lirey, France. It is to honor the Holy Trinity who answered his prayers for a miraculous escape while a prisoner of the English. He is already in possession of the shroud, which some believe he acquired in Constantinople.

1355: The first known expositions of the shroud are held in Lirey around this time. Large crowds of pilgrims are attracted and special souvenir medallions are struck. Bishop Henri refused to believe the shroud could be genuine and ordered the expositions halted. The shroud was then hidden away.

AUGUST 4, 1389: A letter signed by King Charles VI of France orders the bailiff of Troyes to seize the shroud at Lirey and deposit it in another of Troyes' churches pending his further decision about its disposition.

SEPTEMBER 5, 1389: The king's First Sergeant reports to the bailiff of Troyes that "the cloth was now verbally put into the hands of our lord the king."

JUNE 1390: A Papal bull grants new indulgences to those who visit St. Mary of Lirey and its relics.

MAY 22, 1398: Death of Geoffrey II de Charny

JUNE 1418: The widowed daughter of Geoffrey de Charny, Margaret, marries the Count de la Rouche, Lord of St. Hippolyte sur Doubs.

JULY 6, 1418: The Lirey Canons hand over the Shroud to Humbert for safe-keeping. According to seventeenth century chroniclers, annual expositions of the shroud are held at this time in a meadow on the banks of the river Doubs.

MAY 8, 1443: Dean and Canons of Lirey petition Margaret de Charny (de la Rouche) to return the shroud to them.

MARCH 22, 1453: Margaret de Charny, at Geneva, receives from Duke Louis I of Savoy the castle of Varambon and revenues of the estate of Miribel near Lyon for "valuable services." Those services are thought to have been the bequest of the shroud.

FEBRUARY 6, 1464: By an accord drawn up in Paris, Duke Louis I of Savoy agrees to pay the Lirey Canons an annual rent, to be drawn from the revenues of the castle of Gaillard, near Geneva, as compensation for their loss of the shroud. (This is the first surviving document to record that the shroud has become Savoy property.) The accord specifically notes that the shroud had been given to the church of Lirey by Geoffrey de Charnay, lord of Savoisy and Lirey, and that it then had been transferred to Duke Louis by Margaret de Charnay."

But there is something beyond the historical trail of ownership that keeps drawing our attention back to the Middle Ages whenever the Shroud is mentioned. It is the spiritual aspect of the people living during this time. During the medieval period of Shroud history, those involved were not looking for "proof" of any kind, nor did they make demands for any "corroboration." Theirs was a straightforward declaration of faith. It is the veneration of the Shroud during the Middle Ages that provides the clearest picture of what brought the Shroud to the position of special prominence it holds to the present-day.

But in the 20th century, opposition to the authenticity of the Shroud arose. Theories claim that the image on the cloth is a painting, most likely done in the Middle Ages. But do but these theories carry any weight? The next chapter deals with this part of the controversy.

Endnotes

1   Daniel Scavone, PhD., *Mysteries of the Ancient World*, (Banbury, CN: Dell Publishing, 1995), P. 77.

2   Ibid.

3   De Nantes, Georges RP., ed. "The Evidence of a Scientific Forger" *The Catholic Counter Reformation in the XXth Century*, March 1991.

4   Ibid.

5   Ibid.

6   Michael Minor, Esq., Interview, *The Shroud of Turin: Is It the Burial Cloth of Jesus*? DVD, David W. Balsiger, Senior Producer, Grizzly Adams Productions, Inc., 2000.

7   Michael Minor, comp., *The Shroud of Turin: Unraveling the Mystery: Proceedings of the 1998 Dallas Symposium* (Alexander, NC: Alexander Books, 2002), P. 356.

8   Michael Minor, Esq., Interview, *The Fabric of Time*, DVD, David W. Balsiger, Senior Producer, Grizzly Adams Productions, Inc., 2006.

9   Albert Driesbach, Fr., Interview *The Shroud of Turin: Is It the Burial Cloth of Jesus*? DVD, David W. Balsiger, Senior Producer, Grizzly Adams Productions, Inc., 2000.

10   Ibid.

11   Ian Wilson, "Highlights of the Undisputed History," *The Shroud of Turin: The Most Up-To-Date Analysis of All the Facts Regarding the Church's Controversial Relic,* Bernard Ruffin and C. Bernard Ruffin (Grand Rapids: Our Sunday Visitor, 1999), P. 1-3.

SEVEN

THE IMAGE: ART OR ARTIFACT?

An encounter with the Shroud of Turin is unique in several respects. First, as an artifact, there is nothing quite like it anyplace in the world. Second, it is a virtually intact artifact, which means it is subject to objective analysis and scientific evaluation.

At the very heart of this scientific analysis is the question: Is the image on the Shroud some kind of artistic creation or is it a true artifact of the first century? No one doubts that there is an image on the Shroud, but how did it get there? And when? That is the crux of the entire controversy. Perhaps the most prevalent theory about how the image was created is that an artist used the application of paint, dye, powder, or other substance on the cloth after placing the Shroud on a model or statue of a man. Other skeptics have come forward with similar suggestions, adding that heat, acid or some other chemical might have been used to give the image permanence and/or age.

Other ideas give credit for the image to more "natural" causes, such as the diffusion of gases from the body upward onto the burial cloth. According to these theories, the gases would be the result of sweat, decay products, ammonia, blood, and/or burial spices that came in contact with the body. But if the image was created by natural causes, the critics are left with the uncomfortable realization that nothing even remotely like the Shroud image has ever been found associated with any other dead body, or any other burial cloth.

Is It a Brush Painting?

As science became more sophisticated in its abilities to investigate the world around us, scientists applied new technology to the controversy of the Shroud of Turin. One of the most well-known individuals in the scientific controversy of the Shroud is Dr. Walter McCrone and his assertion that the image on the Shroud was "brush painted." McCrone graduated from Cornell University with a PhD in Chemical Microscopy, and as the Director of McCrone Associates (now The McCrone Group) he devoted his life to this direct method of scientific investigation, uncovering in the process a number of high profile artistic forgeries. He wrote a book, *Judgment Day for the Shroud of Turin*, based on his analysis of the Shroud.

Dr. McCrone began his exhaustive study of the Shroud with a stated belief of its authenticity. McCrone claimed he had hoped it would be a genuine artifact. As he peered into his microscope, he quickly became convinced that the Shroud was a painting. His controversial claim is unequivocal:

> "The 'Shroud' was brush painted by an artist."[1]

McCrone said of the evidence he found: "The artist did an excellent job of creating an image that looks to be pretty much anatomically correct. You can find fault with it, the length of the fingers … the length of the arms, but still, artists, even 500 years ago, were able to paint figures that were anatomically correct. [But] if it was the Shroud of Christ, it would have to be made up of embalming materials and blood and other body fluids. … What we found, microscopically, were pigments … pigments used by an artist and a paint medium that was commonly used in the Middle Ages. This proves the Shroud is a painting. A beautiful painting, but nevertheless, the work of an artist."[2]

McCrone's Methods

For his conclusions, Dr. McCrone relied almost exclusively on observations with a polarized light microscope, although he welcomed corroboration from microscopists using the more modern electron microscope. But he was uncompromising about his findings. When former student Raymond Rogers concluded, "The image does not reside in an applied pigment. The reflectance, fluorescence, and chemical characteristics of the Shroud image indicate that the image-recording mechanism involved some cellulose oxidation-dehydration process," Dr. McCrone responded by saying, "I should ask Ray to return his Certificate for successful completion of my course in Polarized Light Miscroscopy that he took in 1959."[3]

In fairness, it should be pointed out that Dr. McCrone and other researchers have not had the actual Shroud to work with. In most cases, their work has had to be accomplished by examining microscopic individual fibers, fibrils, or microscopic particles captured on sticky-tape from the surface of the cloth. Dr. McCrone never saw the Shroud. He had only sticky tape samples to work with that were supplied by Raymond Rogers. These sticky tapes contained, at most, a few hundred fibrils and particles taken from various places on the Shroud. However, almost all the researchers have had to work under the same restrictions and conditions.

Prior to his death, Dr. McCrone even predicted that some future scientist, say around 2279 AD, would completely vindicate his findings. Indeed, he felt that the 1988 Carbon-14 dating results (which we will also examine in some detail) have already vindicated his unyielding assertion that the Shroud image was hand painted by an artist in 1355 AD. (This date was based primarily on the D'Arcis Memorandum.)

Correspondence with Father Rinaldi

Reluctantly, Dr. McCrone passed his disappointing findings along to Father Peter M. Rinaldi, a Catholic priest who was born near Turin. He was a lifelong Shroud researcher and co-founder of the Holy Shroud Guild. Dr. McCrone's report to

Father Rinaldi states, "Visible on the fibers are tiny red-to-orange dots. These dots are iron-oxide pigment identical in shape, size, and composition to jeweler's rouge or the pigment, Venetian red."

This prompted Father Rinaldi to ask Dr. McCrone several questions:

1. Are these dots, this iron-oxide pigment, this jeweler's rouge, this pigment of Venetian red, actually responsible for the entire stain image on the Shroud? For the so-called blood stains too?

2. Assuming that these dots are indeed the coloring agent for the entire image on the Shroud, do we have proof that such a pigment (i.e., jeweler's rouge, Venetian red) was available and used prior to 1353?

3. Have you ever come across anywhere, in pictorial art with production, in which iron oxide, (i.e., jeweler's rouge, Venetian red) was actually used to obtain the same effect we have in the Shroud image, including its negative image?

4. What was the likely technique a would-be artist used in applying iron-oxide pigment (i.e., jeweler's rouge, Venetian red) in order to obtain not only a *negative effect,* but the incredible precision and realism we so admire in the Shroud image, beginning

with the face, including wounds, contusions, flow of blood, etc.?[4]

The *negative effect* is an important point that is often overlooked; the image on the Shroud is actually on the underside of the fabric, or the inside of the fabric, both frontal (front) and dorsal (back), that was next to the body. It is therefore a "mirror" image when viewed from the front.

Dr. McCrone responded to each of Father Rinaldi's questions in detail, and at one point wrote, "Additional studies since readying the enclosed report have changed my ideas a little bit. I thought at first that only a synthetic iron oxide, jeweler's rouge, available only after about 1800, was present on the Shroud. However, I now see evidence for older forms of iron oxide, especially natural iron-oxide pigments that have been used for many hundreds of years."[5]

This was indeed a fortuitous change of mind for Dr. McCrone's study since the image has unquestionably been on the Shroud since at least the fourteenth century, long before the 1800's.

He further explained that he was "still trying to keep Father Rinaldi happy with the idea the Shroud could have been first century and is only enhanced by the red ochre. ... It is extremely important to realize that the iron oxide may be only an enhancement of an earlier image. This we were able to show by counting colored fibers in image areas as compared with colored fibers in non-image areas."[6]

How then does Dr. McCrone explain the negative aspect of the image and the fact of its three-dimensional quality when photographed? In another reply to a letter from Father Rinaldi, who very pointedly asked the same question, Dr. McCrone wrote: "I feel the negative character of the image is a coincidence resulting from the artist's conception of his commission. I feel it is also a coincidence that the 'negative' image yields a three-dimensional figure. This is a natural consequence of the artist's effort to produce a body image based on contact points."[7]

Father Rinaldi repeatedly asked Dr. McCrone to discuss his findings with a qualified art expert, but McCrone steadfastly refused. "My problem with a serious dialogue with qualified art experts," he said, "is finding one I regard as expert." He added, "The Shroud is not a question for art experts."[8]

Artist's Pigment or Cellulose Fibers?

In the meantime, Professor John L. Brown, also a microscopist, but more comfortable with the modern electron microscope, came to exactly the opposite conclusions:

> Walter McCrone believes the image on the Shroud is either a directly painted image or an image perhaps reinforced with artist's pigment. One of the pigments he's identified is iron oxide using optical microscope techniques, but an x-ray fluorescent scan of the entire Shroud shows no more concentration of iron in the image areas than there is on the cloth itself. I don't believe [his] theory because there is so little pigment shown in the image areas on the Shroud, and the image itself only consists of degraded cellulose fibers, which have a yellowish color as seen by the human eye.[9]

Dr. McCrone and others who agree with him stirred up a whole new area of controversy. Can a microscope determine the authenticity of the Shroud of Turin? However, there were those who took a look at Dr. McCrone's studies and took an opposite view.

The Role of STURP

In 1978, the former king of Italy and the Church permitted the Shroud to be examined by a team of prestigious scientists who called themselves The Shroud of Turin Research Project, known simply as STURP. Father Peter Rinaldi was instrumental in obtaining this permission.

Prior to this time Shroud researchers had minimal data for long-distance scientific research, and most of them had never seen the actual Shroud. But now, for the first time, official permission had been given which allowed for open investigation of the Shroud. The assembled group of scientists, under the direction of Tom D'Muhala, arrived in Turin to examine the data around the clock for five days and nights. The team outlined two specific areas of research: 1) Dating the Shroud, and 2) Determining the nature of and information on the Shroud through the use of electron microscopy and neutron activation, radiographic examination, X-ray fluorescence examination, photomicrography, infrared photographs, ultraviolet photographs, color and black and white photographs in whole and in sections.

The data they gathered, including sticky tape samples from the Shroud, has resulted in years of exhaustive study using the most sophisticated instruments and techniques available to modern day space-age science by leading scientific and forensic experts in 92 different disciplines from around the world which have been drawn to the project since that time. As of to date, more than 250,000 man-hours of examining and interpreting the information derived from the Shroud, in an attempt to determine the origins of the haunting image that has lasted through the centuries, has made it the most intensively studied artifact in history. More than 1,000 tests have been conducted, and at least 32,000 photographs have been taken. As a result, what is or is not scientifically acceptable with regard to the Shroud has been largely determined by this team of 40 scientists, working with samples and data gathered from the Shroud, and working mostly independently in universities and laboratories across the United States and abroad. The results of STURP's continued findings are included throughout the chapters of this book.

STURP's official reply to Dr. McCrone's theory is stated in the following chapter, as the controversy continues in the investigative attempts to determine whether the image on the Shroud is an artistic creation or a genuine artifact of the first century.

Endnotes

1   McCrone, Walter, PhD, *Judgment Day for the Shroud of Turin* (Amherst, NY: Prometheus Books, 1999), P. 114.

2   Walter McCrone, Interview, *The Shroud of Turin: Is It the Burial Cloth of Jesus?* DVD, David W. Balsiger, Senior Producer, Grizzly Adams Productions, Inc., 2000.

3   *Judgment Day*, P. 97.

4   Ibid., 110.

5   Ibid., 114.

6   Ibid., 115.

7   Ibid., 204.

8   Ibid.

9   John L. Brown, Prof., Interview, *The Shroud of Turin: Is It the Burial Cloth of Jesus?* DVD, David W. Balsiger, Senior Producer, Grizzly Adams Productions, Inc., 2000.

Eight

WHAT IS A PAINTING?

Dr. McCrone led the way for those who believe that the Shroud of Turin is a work of art, not an artifact. But these opinions were generated by scientists, not artists. Would the view of an art expert differ from that of a scientist? As Dr. McCrone believed the Shroud is a work to be examined by science, Dame Isabel Piczek, an expert in art, represents the view from the artistic world. And she finds Dr. McCrone's theory absurd. "Paint particles," she states emphatically, "are not a painting." From there, she confronts the findings of Dr. McCrone and throws even more controversy into the battle.

A View from the Art World

Scarcely does the world find the rare combination of a highly successful commercial artist also being a particle physicist. Dame Piczek is such a person. Her reputation as an artist, physicist, teacher, and art expert is international in scope. She has created large-scale monumental works of art in 486 buildings around the world. In responding to Dr. McCrone's statements, she addressed specific aspects of his analysis:

> I can assure everyone, the Turin Shroud is not a painting or artifact made by man. The claim was made [by Dr. McCrone] that the Shroud was painted with greatly diluted glue tempera. Glue erratically reacts to atmospheric changes. Therefore, it is used only with chemical stabilizers. If none can be found on the Shroud sticky tapes, it is not a glue paint medium. In much diluted form, the medium does not permanently hold the paint particles. Also, this medium remains absolutely water-soluble. In the case of a highly diluted medium, one does not have to dislodge paint particles. They are loosely attached. Because of the unpleasant qualities of this medium, this technique seldom was used for fine art.[1]

As Dame Piczek meticulously refuted the entirety of Dr. McCrone's arguments, she added:

Our microscopist takes his knowledge of medieval paint techniques from old books, such as Cennino, Cennini, and Eastlake. ... The word *sinopia* or *sinoper* used by McCrone, for instance, is not in use today, and Venetian red is just an arbitrary term used for the unknown *sinoper*. ... The professional arts strongly state, the Shroud is not a painting or man-made artifact. The Shroud is much, much more than anyone of us could even start to understand.[2]

Lacking Artistic Focus

While it is true that microscopic traces of "paint" particles have been found on the cloth, Dr. Piczek is unyielding in her analysis. In addition to the complete lack of any medium to bind these particles to the image, she points to other aspects of the painter's art that are missing as well.

"The Shroud has no light focus," she told us. "Every painting has to have a light focus, meaning that we see in it the direction of the light. ... It seems rather, to obey the laws of geometrical optics. No artist, past, present, or in the future, can or has ever painted like this.

"And it goes even further. The body of the man in the Shroud shows strong and absolutely correct foreshortening without the law of geometrical optics. Anatomical foreshortening was not known by artists before the Renaissance painters, probably a hundred years after the first recorded exhibition of the Shroud, and even then only with the use of the light focus.

"And there's more; the Shroud image has no outlines. Every painting has to have outlines. Even the very paint materials, by their natural edge, create outlines. Again, this is something that goes against the laws of nature, as does the fact that no painting will yield more knowledge than the painter has to put into it, yet the Shroud yields more and more knowledge with each new examination."[3]

Another point stacks the deck against the painting theory: If the Mandylion and the Shroud of Turin are one and the same, the cloth would have had to survive flood, fire, several wars, and 2,000 years of being folded, unfolded, damaged, and repaired. Could a painting made with a highly diluted (water based) glue tempera survive such an ordeal? Especially one painted on a piece of ordinary linen fabric? Could it last 700 years, or 100 years?

In the end, Dr. McCrone convinced no one that the image is a painting but himself and the heirs to the company he founded. In fact, he persistently held his observations and analysis to be superior to some of the world's leading hematologists, nuclear scientists, particle physicists, chemists, biologists, space scientists, computer experts, photographic and fabric specialists, and dozens of other scientific experts. Not one of whom agreed with him.

STURP's Summary

STURP (Shroud of Turin Research Project) also investigated the painting theory. After years of individual and collaborative research by members of the STURP team, representing a broad spectrum of scientific disciplines, the official summary of STURP's findings is explicit:

> After several years of exhaustive study and evaluation of the data, STURP officially concludes: No pigments, paints, dyes, or stains have been found on the fibrils. X-ray fluorescence and microchemistry on the fibrils preclude the possibility of paint being used as a method for creating the image. Ultra-violet and infrared evaluation

confirms these studies. Computer image enhancement and analysis by a device known as a VP-8 Image Analyzer show that the image has unique, three-dimensional information encoded in it.

Microchemical evaluation has indicated no evidence of any spices, oils, or any biochemicals known to be produced by the body in life or in death. It is clear that there has been a direct contact of the Shroud with a body, which explains certain features such as the scourge marks, as well as the blood. However, while this type of contact might explain some of the features of the torso, it is totally incapable of explaining the image of the face with the high resolution, which has been amply demonstrated by photography.

The basic problem from a scientific point of view is that some explanations, which might be tenable from a chemical point of view, are precluded by physics. Contrariwise, certain physical explanations, which may be attractive, are completely precluded by the chemistry. For an adequate explanation for the image of the Shroud, one must have an explanation, which is scientifically sound from a physical, chemical, biological, and medical viewpoint. At the present, this type of solution does not appear to be obtainable by the best efforts of the members of the Shroud Team. Furthermore, experiments in physics and chemistry with old linen have failed to reproduce adequately the phenomenon presented by the Shroud of Turin. The scientific consensus is that the image was produced by something which resulted in oxidation, dehydration, and conjugation of the polysaccharide structure of the microfibrils of the linen itself.

Such changes can be duplicated in the laboratory by certain chemical and physical processes. A similar type of change in linen can be obtained by sulfuric acid or heat. However, there are no chemical or physical methods known which can account for the totality of the image, nor can any combination of physical, chemical, biological, or medical circumstances explain the image adequately.[4]

Another amazing discovery was made through the use of the VP-8 Image Analyzer that is mentioned in STURP's report. While processing the VP-8 photographic image, the scientists found that it had a "wide range of spatial frequencies."[5] This meant that however the image was applied to the cloth, it was completely *random*. The significance of that is that the image could not have been formed by a human hand. It would simply be impossible. No method of applying anything by hand can be directionless.[6] Whatever the image was, or however it was formed it was categorically not a painting.

Where Did the Particles Originate?

Other theorists concede that there are microscopic traces of pigment on the Shroud, but offer a different explanation. According to these experts, the paint pigment found on the Shroud comes from artist-made copies of the Shroud that were touched to the Shroud to gain sanctity for their creations.[7] Thus, particles of paint from the copies would be transferred to the Shroud.

But other researchers totally disagree. Some experts point out that molecular paint traces can be found even in the non-image Shroud areas and contend that these are simply dust particulates acquired over the years. Other qualified scientists argue that the unique effect found on the fibril surfaces cannot be produced by any known paint and far more resemble a radiation burn than any kind of intentional colorization.

Dame Piczek summed up the dilemma this way:

> There are certain paradoxes that the professional artist can see looking at the Shroud that cannot be explained and which a professional artist could not have been doing today, yesterday, or in the Middle Ages.[8]

> While the product of Art fundamentally differs from any other manmade object with its aesthetic merit and its influence on the future, it still visibly manifests that it can only be a human product ... I can assure everyone, the Turin Shroud is not a painting or artifact made by man.[9]

The task of painting the image on the Shroud by any means appears to be beyond any artist's capability. And other critical details are simplistically overlooked by those who wish to credit an artist with painting the image on the cloth. There are no brush strokes anywhere on the fabric. Also, the image itself rests only on the top fibrils of the fibers that make up the cloth. Paint would penetrate into or even seep through the fabric wherever it is applied. There is no such penetration or capillarity.

The DaVinci Theory

Despite the contradictory evidence, the idea that the image on the Shroud must be a painting refuses to go away. In 2005, a major cable TV network produced a documentary showing that not only is the image a painting, it was "most likely" painted by the great Leonardo DaVinci. Dame Piczek thinks the hypothesis is absurd:

There are many lesser arguments, but referring specifically to the notion that Leonardo DaVinci painted the Shroud, it should be obvious that he could not have done so. He was born a hundred years after the first exhibition of the Shroud, and his personal painting techniques are well-known. He was an extremely slow painter, unable to master the techniques of fresco painting. That was the tragedy of The Last Supper, which started to peel during his lifetime. The mural of the Battle of Anghiari started to run and was destroyed while he was still working on it. Unfortunately, most of the great master's works are in a varying state of preservation because of this slow and much layered technique which he employed without exception.

The Shroud has absolutely no paint layers. There is absolutely no chance that Leonardo DaVinci would have or could have painted it, even if it was a painting.

Dame Piczek points out one other historical note: In all of the detailed notebooks kept by Leonardo, who recorded even such minute details as a shoelace he bought for his student Salaino, there is not one drawing, not even a sentence that would hint at any work on a Shroud-like project.[10]

In an attempt to give the theory a veneer of modern science, the network suggested that the art of photography was actually invented for the very purpose of creating the image 600 years before it was a recognized technology. The network then suggested (being very careful not to state factually) that their experiments proved the thesis. But in fact, the experiments were all total failures, proving the exact opposite.

The Leonardo DaVinci theory presents yet another dilemma for those who cling to it: Either the entire history of the Mandylion, which predates DaVinci by hundreds of years, must be discarded or otherwise explained, or one must suppose there were two Shrouds—the one touched by King Abgar and brought by force of arms to Constantinople, and the one painted by DaVinci.

But that isn't the end of the "Shroud is a painting" argument. In September 2006, another major network took its cameras to the McCrone Group. The subjects of the Shroud of Turin and the Vinland Map were raised as major hoaxes uncovered by McCrone's particular brand of microscopy. It wasn't mentioned in the piece that Dr. McCrone had only sticky tape samples to work with that were supplied by his colleague Raymond Rogers. These sticky tapes contained, at most, a few hundred fibrils and particles taken from various places on the Shroud. Nor was it mentioned that Dr. McCrone's thesis about the Vinland Map is in serious dispute by Yale University's several acclaimed experts.

Don Brooks, the CEO of the McCrone Group, told the network reporter that McCrone "obtained and examined 88,000 fibers and particles" in determining that the Shroud was a painting.[11]

The interviewer, apparently having limited knowledge of the subject, never thought to question if "88,000 particles and fibers" wouldn't have taken the entire fabric.

Dame Piczek responded to this most recent attempt by the media to conclusively dismiss the Shroud image as a painting:

> Television program moderators are asking physicists, chemists, medical experts, the corner druggist, and high school teachers this question, and, of course, the answer is always wrong. First and above all, a painting always is the result of an educated, conscious, and intelligent activity. It is never a strange, single item. It faultlessly fits into the cultural era of its time, either as its member or as its consequence, creating the next necessary step. The Turin Shroud does not fit this definition at all.

> In spite of what lay people hold to be true, a painting does not depend on paint particles. It thoroughly and solely depends on the paint *mediums*, binders in liquid forms, mediums that tie the paint particles to each other and to the paint background. This creates a continuous film that alone carries the image consciously willed by the painter to appear on a surface. By natural law, it can only be a visible and continuous image while the medium film remains intact.

Once it starts to disintegrate, chunks of the image or the painting will be missing.

The image on the Turin Shroud is an intact, continuous image without any continuous paint medium film. This is the strongest and most definite proof that the Shroud is not a painting. This very fact alone is enough to kill the "painting" accusation. If an image on a painting could exist without a continuous medium paint film, it would be a greater miracle than the Shroud itself. It would go against all the laws of nature.[12]

When the STURP team published their findings they said that "the actual image was created by a phenomenon (as yet unknown) or a momentous event that caused a rapid cellulose degradation (aging) of the linen fibers, that is, an accelerated dehydration and oxidation of the very top linen fibrils of the cellulose fibers of the Shroud, thereby creating a sepia or straw-yellow colored image similar to that of a scorch."[13]

Therefore, the Shroud is a scientific enigma: It is a piece of cloth containing a surface anomaly in the shape and form of a crucified man, created by some totally unknown process that apparently occurred after a large number of blood stains had exuded onto the cloth.

With the controversy heating up, the interest in the Shroud of Turin heightened. Many scientists from other disciplines also examined the Shroud of Turin. With their modern technological advancements, they made some astounding discoveries.

Endnotes

1   Dame Isabel Piczek, "The Professional Arts and the Principle and Practice of Conservation Restoration vs. the Turin Shroud," *Proceedings of the 1999 International Research Conference,* Brian J. Walsh ed. (Richmond, VA: Magisterium Press, 2000), P. 85-87, 93.

2   Ibid.

3   Dame Isabel Piczek, Interview, *The Fabric of Time,* DVD. David W. Balsiger, Senior Producer, Grizzly Adams Productions, Inc., 2006.

4   "A Summary of STURP's Conclusions," The 1978 Scientific Examination, 25 February 2007, <http://www.Shroud.com/78conclu.htm.>

5   *John Heller,* PhD, MD, "Report on the Shroud of Turin," *Mysteries of the Ancient World* (Banbury, CN: Dell Publishing, 1995), P. 85, 86.

6   Ibid., ref. to an article in the Scientific Journal, *Science.*

7   Albert Driesbach, Fr., Interview, *Shroud of Turin: Is It the Burial Cloth of Jesus?* DVD, David W. Balsiger, Senior Producer, Grizzly Adams Productions, Inc., 2000.

8   Dame Isabel Piczek, PhD, Interview, *The Shroud of Turin: Is It the Burial Cloth of Jesus?* DVD, David W. Balsiger, Senior Producer, Grizzly Adams Productions, Inc., 2000.

9   Dame Isabel Piczek, "The Professional Arts," P. 82, 85.

10 Dame Isabel Piczek, *The Fabric of Time.*

11 Walter McCrone, PhD, *Judgment Day for the Shroud of Turin,* (Amherst, NY: Prometheus Books, 1999).

12 Dame Isabel Piczek, *The Shroud of Turin.*

13 John C. Iannone, *The Mystery of the Shroud of Turin* (NY: Alba House, 1998), 15.

NINE

POKED, PRODDED, AND ANALYZED

In Paris, on Sunday the 25th of November, 1990, a group of Catholic parishioners assembled to hear a series of lectures on the Shroud. In his opening remarks, the Abbé Georges de Nantes stood before this dedicated gathering and said:

> Ours is the truth, whatever the cost. There is no halfway between the first and fourteenth centuries, between authenticity and fraud. The image and blood of this cloth are either a divine miracle or a human imposture. They are either the work of a villainous and blasphemous lie motivated by lucre, or else they are the extraordinary result of a number of scientifically discernible causes.[1]

Abbé Nantes summarized the motive for truth underlying the efforts of the scholars and scientists who have examined the Shroud of Turin. Most investigators, critics and supporters alike, would probably agree that if we could determine precisely how the image got on the cloth, everything else would become quite clear. For nearly thirty years now, a concerted scientific effort has been underway to make that determination.

Dr. McCrone and his colleagues were not the only scientists doing tests on the Shroud during this time period. Scientists from many different scientific fields brought their expertise to the table, and their results prompted intriguing explanations. These theories deserve our attention.

Suggested Theories

In his book, *The Resurrection of the Shroud*, St. Louis attorney Mark Antonacci describes and refutes each of the more prominent theories suggested for how the image could have been created in the Middle Ages.

One of the earliest theories he addresses is the "Vapograph" theory, proposed by Paul Vignon, one of the first scientists to study the Shroud around the turn of the twentieth century, which suggests that the image was formed by vapors. Antonacci concludes that this theory cannot be possible because the image is found only on the topmost fibrils of the linen thread. Vapors would necessarily penetrate into and between the threads of the linen.

A Shroud of Turin Research Project (STURP) scientist, Sam Pellicori, is one of several researchers to suggest that the image was caused by direct-contact with a body covered with "… perspiration, body oils, and/or liquid solutions of myrrh, aloes, or olive oil;" however, no traces of these types of organic liquid substances have been detected on the linen.[2] Antonacci adds that this method would not have allowed the image to produce the three-dimensional information found in the Shroud, as well as the facial details of the image.[3] Therefore, the Pellicori theory of how the image got on the Shroud is invalid.

Another theory, referred to as the "Volkringer Method," is suggested by a Paris pharmacist who thought the image might have been created in a manner similar to the way the image of leaves or flowers is imprinted on paper when pressed between the pages of a book. However, pressing a body between cloth would leave decomposition stains, which are not found on the Shroud of Turin.[4]

The "Singlet Oxygen Theory," postulates a combination of all these theories. A woven piece of linen, however, is not sensitive like a photography glass plate, and will not record impressions easily. Yet, the Shroud has many delicate images of flowers besides the images of the body.[5] This renders the possibility of the Singlet Theory as impossible.

The "powder rubbing theory" is also summarized, as well as various heat and scorch theories. Antonacci writes:

> The Shroud contains, conservatively, thousands of individual body-image fibrils, but each fibril is encoded with a uniform intensity of color. Someone applying powdered pigment onto a cloth with a hand-held dauber and /or rubbing powder on woven linen could never achieve this uniform intensity on all image fibrils. In fact, experiments involving powder rubbing have shown that a uniform application of powder cannot be obtained on even one fibril.[6]

Each of these various theories attempting to explain the formation of the Shroud image is demonstrated to be flawed, when probed by bona fide scientific analysis.

The Blood Stains

Another particularly sensitive point of discussion with scientists on both sides of the issue revolves around what appear to be blood stains. The question arises: Are the stains actually blood? The controversy on that point was raised to new heights in 1973 when Dr. Georgio Feache at the University of Modena in Italy tested blood stained threads from the Shroud in a chemical solution of benzidine. The test failed to prove the stains were blood.

The experts were at odds with each other. Nothing about the Shroud has been more elaborately tested than the "blood stains." They are a redish-brown color and are separate from the image. Where these stains exist, the image is missing, which means the stains would have to have been on the cloth before the image was formed. They range from the puncture wounds in the head and scalp to the numerous marks of flagellation, to the wounds in the wrists and feet, to the blood flows from the spear wound on the anatomical right side.

The question posed is: Are they actual blood stains, or could they be paint as Dr. McCrone opined? The question is partially answered by simple X-ray. When X-rayed, paint shows up quite distinctively, but X-rays of the Shroud do not show these characteristics. This indicates that the spots could not be paint—at least not any paint that has ever been known. But can we be sure the spots are blood?[7]

Fluorescence studies have been used by several researchers to determine the authenticity of the marks, stains, and images on the cloth, including the blood stains. In 1978, in one particularly intriguing examination, the fluorescence studies discovered an anomaly, the significance of which wouldn't be realized until 2005.

The burns and scorches on the cloth are readily accounted for by the well-known fire in 1532 AD that nearly destroyed the Shroud, and provide a benchmark of sorts when examining the fabric under ultra-violet light. The scorches give off an orange fluorescence while the body images do not fluoresce at all.

According to the late Dr. Alan Adler, a world recognized authority on porphyrins and a blood analysis expert, "This observation specifically rules against iron oxides as the body image chromophore, since at the microlevel, the color of the body image fibers is a straw yellow. The only known forms of iron oxides that are this color [straw yellow] are hydrated ferrous forms, which therefore would be discolored by the fire."[8]

Prior to his death, Dr. Alan Adler devoted his Shroud research almost exclusively to the so-called blood stains. His conclusion was that these stains were indeed blood, and furthermore, it was blood loaded with bilirubin, a blood component that would be present in large quantities only if the victim had been scourged, tortured, or died a violent death.

According to Dr. Adler, "All of the medical forensic examinations of the blood images are in agreement that they were [exuded] from clotted wounds transferred to the cloth by its being in contact with a wounded human male body, consistent with the historic descriptions given for the Crucifixion of Christ."[9]

In other words, the blood images got on the cloth precisely the same way a person gets blood on a handkerchief when he has a bloody nose. But Dr. Adler's research produced another more profound discovery; the image is *not* present under the blood stains.

According to Dr. Adler, "Enzymatic removal of the blood from a blood-coated fiber reveals that the blood got on the cloth first and therefore protected the blood covered areas of the cloth from the image-forming process. All the microscopic, chemical, spectroscopic, and immunological evidence is consistent with these images, not only being exudated from clotted wounds, but those of a man who suffered severe trauma prior to death, explaining the red color of the blood at the microscopic level."[10]

Dr. McCrone dismissed the work of Dr. Adler, saying simply, "There is *no* [his emphasis] blood on the Shroud." And he added, "Obviously, I amuse myself by thinking of Heller [another proponent of authenticity] and Adler, 'STURP shroudies,' who found blood everywhere on the Shroud."[11]

But ultraviolet photography reveals yet another fact about the Shroud that argues against almost any kind of manmade image. Dr. Adler pointed out:

Every single blood wound shows a distinct serum clot retraction ring. ... It is clear that we can explain the presence of the blood images on the cloth consistent with their alleged origin. Any attempt to explain the formation of the body images must take these properties of the blood images into account. One cannot simply say that the blood images were painted on afterwards. One would need a constant supply of fresh clot exudates from a traumatically wounded human to paint in all the forensically correct images in the proper non-stereo register and then finally paint a serum contraction ring about every wound. Logic suggests that this is not something a forger or artisan before the present century would not only know how to do, but even know that it was required.[12]

One particular test is formidable proof. Samples from the blood-stained Shroud were taken to Yale University where Dr. John Heller and his associate, Dr. Alan Adler, not only determined that the so-called blood stains on the Shroud were indeed blood but, as Dr. Adler reiterated in his presentation at the Shroud of Turin International Research Conference in 1999, blood and sera highly loaded with bilirubin, a bile pigment that would show up only if the dead man had been either jaundiced, or severely and horribly beaten.

Meanwhile, across the ocean, working completely independent of Heller and Adler, the noted pathologist and professor, Dr. Pierluigi Balma Bollone, came to the conclusion that the blood spots on the Shroud were not only human, but were type AB. With regard to Dr. Bollone's findings, Dr. McCrone's attitude was even more cavalier than it was with Dr. Adler. "Dr. Bollone," he says, "is appropriately named."[13]

Photographic Negative

Some scientists suggested that a type of photographic technique was employed in creating the image. But professional photographers do not think that idea has any merit. In his booklet, *The Images on the Shroud*, Nello Ballosino explains:

An extraordinary characteristic of the Shroud, photographically speaking, is its "negativity." The imprints behave like a photographic negative, (except for the blood stains which are in positive). We know that if we photograph something, we get the "photographic negative" on the film, i.e., an image that presents light and shade combinations completely reversed, and also spatial transposition, which changes left to right and vice versa. From the negative, we get photographs, which reproduce the object as originally seen."[14]

The Flowers and Pollen

Researchers also began questioning if there was anything on the fabric that gave clues to its origin. The Gospel of John tells us:

> At the place where Jesus was crucified there was a garden, and in the garden a new tomb, in which no one had ever been laid (John 19:41, NIV).

This tiny bit of information provides a tantalizing clue as to whether or not this could actually be the burial cloth of Jesus. In his exhaustive research on the Shroud image, Dr. Whanger zeroed in on this detail:

> We had noted the presence of other objects on the Shroud besides the body, and we found, to our astonishment, the highly accurate images of many flowers, actually many hundreds of these, but we were able to identify 28 species with what we feel is a good degree of accuracy. The importance of this is these flowers all grow either in Jerusalem or within 12 miles of Jerusalem. In addition, the pollens of 25 of these flowers that we've found have also been independently identified on the Shroud. Whatever produced the image of the body,

which some feel is the Resurrection, also produced a high energy field producing images of every object that was in the Shroud, and hence we have highly accurate images of these flowers.[15]

Could it be that while Jesus' followers were anointing the body of Jesus and wrapping it in the grave cloth purchased by Joseph of Arimathea, the women who followed them gathered flowers from the garden and placed them around the body? Scripture tells us only that the women followed Joseph and Nicodemus to the tomb where Jesus was laid (Luke 23:55). The Shroud itself suggests that flowers may have been harvested from the garden nearby as well as brought from local fields or markets and placed within the Shroud with Jesus' body.

In 1973, the Shroud was brought out for a brief examination by a group of European scientists. Among them was the late Dr. Max Frei, a Swiss botanist and criminalist, and one of the world's leading experts in dust and pollen analysis. With the support of the Turin Shroud authorities, Dr. Frei was allowed to use sticky tapes to take pollen samples from the Shroud and compare them with pollen archives of Palestinian and Near Eastern plants.

During this gathering of pollen samples, Frei found what he believed were pollens from plants which grow only in Turkey.[16] That would account for the presence of the Shroud in Edessa, (now part of Eastern Turkey), but Dr. Frei was more definitive:

> The pollen grains confirmed the presence of the Shroud in Turkey, but that isn't all I have found. I saw many other specimens which I couldn't identify by the help of botanical textbooks. So I had to travel personally to such countries as the Shroud might have been in. It was quite natural to go first to Jerusalem and the surrounding regions of Judea. Here I found the answer ... plants in [a] particular variety ... known only in Palestine. I found pollens from [them] on the Shroud.[17]

At first glance, Dr. Frei's objective was simple: If the Shroud was forged in France in the fourteenth century, only French or Italian pollens would be found on the cloth. But his exhaustive analysis found dozens of different species of pollens, only 17 of which were indigenous to Europe. The rest were from plants that grow in Palestine and southern Turkey, the sites of Edessa and

Constantinople. This of course meant the Shroud had been in those places at some time in its history.

According to Professor Silvano Scannerini, author of *Myrrh, Aloes, Pollen, and Other Traces*, "These pollens have provided some interesting clues to the Shroud's history, being substantially in agreement with the popular and religious tradition as regards the Shroud."[18]

There was yet another surprise in store for those examining the flower images, one that appears to confirm the biblical account of the Crucifixion in an even more specific way. Dr. Avinoam Danin, Professor of Botany at Hebrew University in Jerusalem and author of the definitive textbook of the flora and fauna of Israel, began to examine the images more closely. He made an amazing discovery. "One of these flowers has a unique characteristic. It is tightly closed in the morning but opens slowly throughout the day. By its position on the Shroud, we can say with some certainty that it was placed with the body at approximately four in the afternoon."[19]

If Dr. Danin's analysis is correct, he has provided proof that the Shroud was wrapped around the body at the very hour that the

Bible says the body was buried, just before Sabbath or before twilight.

VP-8 Image Analyzer

The light and electron microscopes, Carbon-14 dating, chemical analysis, fluorescent lighting, special photography, pollen analysis and modern criminology methods are but a sampling of an impressive array of scientific weapons available in the modern scientific arsenal. But one of the most significant in revealing unprecedented Shroud discoveries, the VP-8 Image Analyzer, came on the scene in the 1970s. Technically, the VP-8 Image Analyzer is an analog video processing device. It projects an isometric display, which is generated on a cathode ray tube, like that of an oscilloscope much like a home television set, except the scanning and positioning of the video image are controlled by voltages rather than electromagnetism.

Originally intended to help space scientists explore terrain features on far off planets by analyzing the varying shades of gray being returned by signals from orbiting satellites, the VP-8 Analyzer can vary the elevation scale (Z axis) relative to the X and Y axis scale.

The isometric display uses the changes of brightness as they occur in an image, to change the "elevation" on the display. If something is bright, it goes up. If something is dark, it goes down. If it is some gray shade in between, it produces an elevation in-between something very bright and something very dark.[20]

In 1976, Peter M. Schumacher, the man responsible for taking the VP-8 Analyzer design to production and delivery, was asked to deliver and install a unit at the home of Captain Eric Jumper, USAF. Schumacher installed the VP-8, verified the calibration, and then trained Jumper and others in the operation of the system. According to Schumacher, what happened next was extraordinary.

"An image [photo] of the Shroud of Turin was placed onto the light table of the system and the video camera was focused on the image. When the pseudo-three-dimensional image display (i.e., isometric display) was activated, a true three-dimensional image appeared on the monitor; the nose ramped in relief; the facial features were contoured properly. Body shapes of the arms, legs, and chest had the basic human form. *This result from the VP-8 had never occurred with any other images"* [emphasis added].[21]

Later, scientists from the original STURP group also put the Shroud image to the test. Like Schumacher, they found the three-dimensional information stunning and so accurate they were actually able to create a three-dimensional, perfectly proportioned statue from the data.

The search for the truth now sprang to a new dimension, and serious scientists suddenly found themselves seated among dedicated theologians who had come to the party years earlier.

Shumacher wrote: "I had never heard of the Shroud of Turin before that moment; however, the results are unlike anything I have processed through the VP-8 Analyzer, before or since. If one considers the Shroud image to be a 'work of art' of some type, then one must consider how and why an artist would embed three-dimensional information in the gray shading of an image. In fact, no means of viewing this property of the image would be available for at least six hundred and fifty years after it was done. One would have to ask, (assuming this is a 'natural result' in some style or type of art), 'Why isn't this result obtained in the analysis of other works?' Or, if this is a unique work, 'Why would the artist make only one such work requiring such special skills and talent, and not pass the technique along to others?' How could the artist control the quality of the work when the artist could not 'see' the gray scale as elevation?"[22]

Schumacher finds the plethora of explanations and conclusions that have been offered since the discovery of this unique characteristic unconvincing at best. "I have heard of no sound explanation," he says, "as to how the Shroud image can be fabricated through any known means or technology."[23]

Forensic Analysis

Researchers went even further in their investigation. They wanted to test if the image on the Shroud could stand up to professional forensic analysis.

The late Dr. Robert Bucklin, a former coroner and Forensic Pathologist for Los Angeles County, was well acquainted with images of violent death and did an extensive and detailed analysis of the image. After a careful examination of a full life-size image of the Shroud, Dr. Bucklin provided the following analysis:

> This is the body of a five-foot, eleven-inch Caucasian male weighing about a hundred and seventy pounds. On the head there are blood flows resulting from numerous puncture wounds on the front, the back, and the top of the head. There's a swelling over one cheek consistent with a beating. The right wrist is covered by the left hand. There's a puncture wound in the left wrist. The classical, artistic, and legendary portrayal of nails through the palms is incorrect. The structures in the hand are too fragile to hold up the weight of a man this size without tearing free.

> There are streams of blood running down both forearms originating in the wrist areas and controlled by gravity. The blood flows toward the elbows, with the arms elevated and outstretched. On the back, there are more than one hundred lesions, which appear to be scourge or whip marks. Historians have indicated that the Romans used a whip called a *flagrum*. This implement had two or three thongs, and at their ends were pieces of metal or bone

which look like small dumbbells. Those end pieces from a Roman *flagrum* fit precisely into the scourge lesions on the body.

On the front of the body is a large blood stain resulting from puncture of the chest by an instrument like a lance or a spear. This weapon penetrated the thoracic cavity and into the heart. Later, after the corpse was removed from the cross and turned, blood dribbled out of the chest wound and puddled along the small of the back.

Finally, nails have been driven through both feet and blood leaked from those areas and has stained the cloth. The evidence of a scourged man who was crucified and who died of postural asphyxia and pulmonary failure is clear cut.

But more than that, this image appears to match perfectly the description of the Crucifixion of Jesus Christ, even adding some detail not included in the Gospels, but conforming perfectly to Jewish law and customs of the time.[24]

Dr. John Heller, a biophysicist, wrote that his interest in the Shroud was first stirred by the report of Dr. Robert Bucklin. Dr. Heller's own interpretation of the forensic findings was direct and to the point:

> Irrespective of how the images were made, there is adequate information here to state that they are anatomically correct. There is no problem in diagnosing what happened to this individual. The pathology and physiology are unquestionable and represent medical knowledge unknown 150 years ago.[25]

The circumstantial evidence to this point supports the authenticity of the Shroud of Turin. The weight of the evidence from the "art or artifact" controversy seems to be tipping the scales to the conclusion that the image is artifact rather than a painting. But this doesn't end the controversy. Another scientific method of examining artifacts produced grave doubts that the Shroud of Turin is authentic—that test method is Carbon-14 dating and the result produced more furor in the journey to find the truth.

Endnotes

1   R.P. Georges de Nantes, ed. "The Holy Shroud" The Catholic Counter-Reformation in the XXth Century, March 1991

2   Mark Antonacci, *The Resurrection of the Shroud* (NY: M. Evans & Company, NY, 2000), P. 61-85.

3   Ibid., 63.

4   Ibid., 68.

5   Ibid., 69.

6   Ibid., 74.

7   Daniel Scavone, PhD, *Mysteries of the Ancient World* (Banbury, CN: Dell Publishing, 1995), P. 93.

8   Alan Adler, PhD, "The Nature of the Body Images on the Shroud of Turin." *Proceedings of the 1999 Shroud of Turin Research Conference,* Brian J. Walsh ed. (Richmond, VA, Magisterium Press, 2000). P. 19.

9   Ibid., 20.

10 Ibid.

11 Walter McCrone, *Judgment Day for the Shroud of Turin* (Prometheus Books, 1999), P. 106, 107.

12 Alan Adler, proceeding of the 1999 Shroud of Turin Research Conference, P. 21.

13 Ibid., 29.

14 Nello Ballosino, *The Image on The Shroud,* Alan Neame, trans. (London, St. Pauls, 1998),

P. 5, 6, 44.

15 Alan Whanger, PhD, Interview, *Shroud of Turin: Is It the Burial Cloth of Jesus?* DVD, David W. Balsiger, Senior Producer, Grizzly Adams Productions, Inc., 2000.

16 Silvano Scannerini, *Myrrh, Aloes, Pollen and Other Traces*, Alan Neame, trans. (London, St. Pauls, 1998), P. 49.

17 Dr. Max Frei, Interview, *Shroud of Turin: Is It the Burial Cloth of Jesus?* DVD, Grizzly Adams Productions, Inc., 2000.

18 Scannerini, P. 51.

19 Alan Whanger, PhD, *Shroud of Turin.*

20 Peter M. Schumacher, "Photogrammetric Responses From the Shroud of Turin." *Proceedings of the 1999 Shroud of Turin International Research Conference.* Brian J. Walsh, ed. (Richmond, VA, Magisterium Press, 2000), P. 32.

21 Ibid., 30.

22 Ibid., 32, 33.

23 Ibid., 34.

24 Robert Bucklin, MD, Interview, *Shroud of Turin: Is It the Burial Cloth of Jesus?* DVD, David W. Balsiger, Senior Producer, Grizzly Adams Productions, Inc., 2000.

25 John Heller, PhD, MD, "Report on the Shroud of Turin," *Mysteries of the Ancient World* (Banbury, CN: Dell Publishing, 1995), P. 85, 86.

TEN

THE CARBON-14 TESTS

One of the great unanswered mysteries of the Shroud of Turin is its age. In spite of all the scientific findings, the historic record, and the uncanny parallels of the image to the Crucifixion of Jesus Christ, a large body of scientific and academic opinion about its age was withheld pending the outcome of Carbon-14 tests on the fabric of the Shroud. Since the process of Carbon-14 testing involves the destruction of the sample, officials of the Catholic Church were reluctant to sacrifice even the small portion necessary to do the testing.

Finally in 1988, after ten long years of discussion and negotiation, three independent laboratories were selected to perform Carbon-14 dating analysis. The tests were authorized and protocols established by the Turin Commission. All tests were to be supervised by the British Museum.

The results proved disappointing to supporters of the Shroud's authenticity and raised the controversy to a new level of controversy. Much of the acrimony generated by the test results and the way the tests were conducted still rages.

The Shroud Declared a Hoax

On October 14, 1988, a press conference was held at the British Museum where the Shroud was declared to be of medieval origin by Dr. Michael Tite, director of the British Museum research laboratory at that time. He was accompanied by Professor Edward Hall, then Director of the Research Laboratory for Archaeology and History of Art at Oxford University, and by physicist Robert Hedges. Dr. Tite had the unenviable task of delivering the results:

> Carbon-14 dating analysis conducted on the Shroud of Turin at three separate laboratories in the United States, England, and Switzerland produced radiocarbon dates ranging from AD 1260 to 1340, about thirteen hundred years shy of being the possible burial cloth of Christ.[1]

After nearly a hundred years of historic and scientific investigation, which tended to support the authenticity of the Shroud, one modern scientific test appeared to contradict all the work that had gone before. The reaction from both sides was predictable.

The case seemed to be closed, but was it?

Beyond a Reasonable Doubt

Michael Minor, a practicing attorney, former prosecutor, and author, was quick to remind everyone: "There are literally thousands of pieces of scientific data to support the conclusion that the Shroud is not a fake or a forgery; however, only one piece of evidence, the Carbon-14 dating, indicates the Shroud is of medieval origin. In my professional opinion, the authenticity of the Shroud can be proven in a court of law beyond a reasonable doubt based on the overwhelming circumstantial evidence."[2]

Other Shroud researchers were critical of the Shroud's authenticity. The news conference resulted in an outpouring of articles asserting the Shroud was obviously a forgery. But according to those who had seen, touched, and tested the Shroud, nothing could be further from the truth. Understandably, they were reluctant to set aside all of the findings that demonstrated the

Shroud to be a genuine burial garment and not a painted fraud. However, even though the Carbon-14 tests, as they pointed out, were fraught with scientific procedure problems, most people accepted the dating without question, and a skeptical press leaped to its own conclusions.[3]

Dr. Tite, unmoved by any of the arguments, steadfastly maintained that the Carbon-14 tests were reliable, stating, "None of the other methods or techniques is actually providing a date. You can infer a date from the results obtained, but none of them provides you with an absolute date. That's why one sees Carbon-14 as different from all the other techniques."[4]

Scientists involved with the Carbon-14 dating procedures found themselves in direct opposition to scientists of virtually every other scientific discipline with Dr. Tite and Dr. Hall caught at the vortex of the storm. Accusations of scientific fraud were leveled, including a suggestion that the Shroud sample had been switched with the sample from a mummy.[5]

In November 1990, Dr. Tite and Dr. Hall were invited to attend a Catholic symposium in Paris to hear the charges and respond to them. Their replies are indicative of the level of acrimony that had arisen over the Carbon-14 test results. Dr. Hall's reply reads:

> Dear Sir,
> I do not waste my time discussing serious matters with people who are bigoted. I will not be coming to Paris in November, at which time you are welcome to make these sentiments known. As far as I am concerned, the matter is closed.
> Yours Sincerely, for
> E.T. Hall[6]

Dr. Tite's response was civil but expressed the same disdain for any suggestion that the Carbon-14 tests were not decisive.

> Dear Brother Bruno:
> In response to your letter of 13 October, I write to confirm that I remain fully convinced that the radiocarbon dates of the Shroud of Turin as presented by the February 1989 issue of *Nature* are valid.
> Yours Sincerely,
> M.S. Tite[7]

By-Passed Protocol

Arguments questioning the validity of Dr. Tite's and Dr. Hall's conclusions do not all come from theologians. Based on his own scientific analysis of the image, Dr. John Jackson also has difficulty with the Carbon-14 results. "The image features that you see on the Shroud align vertically with the corresponding body parts," he wrote, "so in other words, it's as if the image transfer went from the body to the cloth in a vertically upward direction. What mechanism acts this way ... that acts in a vertical-only direction like this? Yet if you accept at face value the Carbon-14 interpretation, this hypothetical someone in the fourteenth-century was able to either know of or involuntarily use a process that creates an image with these characteristics. It's not at all clear to twentieth-century science what it was that caused this image to occur on the Shroud."[8]

Part of the difficulty stems from the fact that the protocols established for the Carbon-14 test and agreed to by the interested parties was changed at the last minute without the changes being announced. The original plan was for each of the three testing laboratories to receive their sample taken from a different spot on the Shroud. Each laboratory would also receive a "control" sample from fabric of a known date, but that date would be "blind" to the testing laboratory. Each lab would test both samples, and a valid comparison could then be made as to the accuracy of each laboratory's test procedures.

Unfortunately, that didn't happen. To conserve the fabric, only a single sample was taken from the Shroud and divided into the three pieces necessary for the three separate tests. The control samples were provided, but for some unknown reason, each laboratory was also given the date of the control sample. So much for a blind comparison.

As Don Lynn, scientist at NASA's Jet Propulsion Laboratory in Pasadena, California, revealed, "They really only tested one area … they didn't do three tests; they did one test three times."[9]

Another Anomaly

Shroud historian, Ian Wilson, uncovered another anomaly of the Shroud that casts doubt on the accuracy of the Carbon-14 tests. Largely unnoticed in the broader scope of the Shroud tests, this anomaly has to do with the damage that the Shroud sustained, which bears directly on the Carbon-14 result. According to Wilson:

> In a painting of 1516, we see marks we can still see as triple holes, as I call them; they look like little burn marks or puncture marks that have been punched into the cloth that clearly show up in a painting of the cloth in 1516 before the 1532 fire. And to see these same little holes depicted on [a] manuscript of 1192 suggests that again we are seeing clear indication of the presence in the history of that time, well before the carbon dating, indicated the presence of the cloth we now know as the Shroud of Turin.[10]

It is an interesting question: How could a document, produced in 1192, contain marks or features found on a Shroud that, according to the Carbon-14 test, didn't exist for another two centuries?

Part of the answer may lie in the apparent willingness of people and the press to accept as valid anything that comes under the rubric of "science." Many researchers point out that Carbon-14 dating is far from an exact science. For example, freshly killed mollusks show they have been dead for 3000 years while bristle cone pine, the oldest trees on Earth, always date too young by two to three thousand years.[11]

Reliability of Tests Questioned

Other odd occurrences having to do with the science of Carbon-14 testing keep turning up. For example, the carbon dating of a Nixon campaign button found along the berm of the Pennsylvania turnpike revealed its age to be between 100 and 120 *million* years. We know, of course, the reason for that was that the dating was reading the fossil-fuel age of the gasoline emissions on the button. For many scientists, carbon dating is not always a dependable test and certainly not in the case of the Shroud.[12]

This may be a crucial point to the Shroud's testing: What is the effect of outside influences on an object being subjected to Carbon-14 testing? At the 1993 Shroud conference in Rome, Italy, Dr. Dimitri A. Kouznetsov, a specialist in physical-chemical research at the Moscow State Center for Sanitation and Ecology Studies, presented a paper on his "Fire Model" theory:

It is known that the Shroud was nearly destroyed in a fire, which occurred in 1532. The Shroud was kept in a silver casket of which the top melted and burned through the Shroud. Silver melts at nine hundred degrees centigrade. By simulating the environment of the fire, which would have been rich in carbon dioxide and carbon monoxide, Kouznetsov was able to show that the linen will absorb up to forty-percent more Carbon-14 from the surrounding carbon-rich gases. This is referred to as "isotopic change." Kouznetsov sharply criticized the carbon labs involved in the 1988 carbon dating tests. Taking account of … these variables would establish an age of the Shroud at no less than nineteen hundred years, or first century.[13]

And what of the control samples that were tested by the three labs? Upon investigating, the investigators turned up some interesting results. Three labs were selected to perform the Carbon-14 tests. They were given three control samples to test. One sample was a piece of bull mummy linen, the oldest of the samples, and already known to be from 3000 BC! The three lab results on this piece of cloth varied from 3440 to 4517 BC, a variance of

1100 years. On the other samples, the range of error was from 4359 to 1500 years. The testers defended the errors as due to contamination of the samples. But after extensive retesting, the oldest sample was still some one thousand years off ... on the young side.[14]

The Presence of Variables

Carbon-14 testing is far from accurate. There are too many variables that can affect the outcome, as in the case of the Nixon button. Many of those variables were either overlooked or ignored in the testing involving the Shroud. For example, no testing or physical measurements were conducted on the site from which the sample was taken. There was no attempt to determine if that area of the Shroud had been damaged or altered in any way by the fire of 1532. STURP recommended that five samples be taken from throughout the cloth and not from or near a patch, scorched area, or reworked area. These conditions were ignored, and the sample was taken from a scorched, patched, and rewoven area of the Shroud.[1*]

1 * NOTE: The labs were not at fault here. They simply followed their normal procedure for Carbon-14 testing using the materials that were ultimately given to them.

These scorched areas and the fire of 1532 took on new significance relative to the Carbon-14 tests when preservation and conservation was done on the Shroud in 2002 under the direction of the world-renowned textile expert, Dr. Mechthild Flury-Lemburg. According to Flury-Lemburg, the work done to restore the Shroud in 2002 was required to arrest noticeable degradation above all the patches, which the Poor Clare Nuns of Chambéry had painstakingly labored nearly five centuries ago to stitch in place in order to repair the damage of the 1532 fire.[15]

The patches covering the holes that resulted from the fire were carefully removed; the carbon residue around the holes that had broken away was meticulously brushed away and preserved. When the Holland cloth backing was removed, it was found that thick dirt deposits of fiber dust had accumulated along the stitch lines. All the particles that had been absorbed over the years were carefully collected. They were stored in small containers with their exact locations noted.

To the naked eye, all the carbon dust appeared to have been removed with the first cleaning, but under a video microscope, traces of carbon dust were still very much in evidence. A second cleaning was necessary.[16]

What is the relevance of the carbon dust in regard to Carbon-14 tests? Assuming for the moment that Kouznetsov was correct and the linen will absorb up to forty-percent more Carbon-14 due to "isotopic change" produced by surrounding carbon, Flury-Lemburg's work suggests that the carbon dust that was cleaned from around the burn holes was likely to have permeated the entire fabric. In a private conversation with Flury-Lemburg at the Shroud Symposium in Turin, Italy, in May 2006, she stated that the Shroud had either been folded or rolled upon itself for hundreds of years and that it would be virtually impossible for the whole fabric *NOT* to have been affected. Thus any portion of the contaminated Shroud would carbon test to essentially the same date.[17]

And so the controversy rages on. Science, rather than solving the mystery, has only added more fuel to the fire. But both sides agree on one thing—more Carbon-14 tests should be performed with stricter adherence to the testing criteria. This, of course, will cause further damage to the Shroud, and thus far the committee has been reluctant to agree to additional destructive testing.

There is, however, one other possibility that until recently was completely overlooked by those on both sides of the argument. What if somehow the Carbon-14 tests and all of the other scientific and historic test results are <u>*all correct*</u>? That possibility is the subject of the next chapter.

Endnotes

1   Michael Tite, PhD, "The Scientific Shroud," *Mysteries of the Ancient World* (Banbury, CN: Dell Publishing, 1995), P. 96.

2   Michael Minor, JD, *The Shroud of Turin: Is It the Burial Cloth of Jesus?* DVD, Grizzly Adams Productions, Inc., 2000.

3   Kenneth Stevenson, Interview, *The Shroud of Turin: Is It the Burial Cloth of Jesus?* DVD, Grizzly Adams Productions, Inc., 2000.

4   Michael Tite, PhD, Interview, *The Shroud of Turin: Is It the Burial Cloth of Jesus?* DVD, Grizzly Adams Productions, Inc., 2000.

5   Georges de Nantes, RP, ed., "The Evidence of a Scientific Forger," *The Catholic Counter Reformation in the XXth Century*, (March 1991:1-9).

6   Ibid. 3.

7   Ibid. 4.

8   John Jackson, PhD, Interview, *The Shroud of Turin: Is It the Burial Cloth of Jesus?* DVD, Grizzly Adams Productions, Inc., 2000.

9   Don Lynn, Interview, *The Shroud of Turin: Is It the Burial Cloth of Jesus?* DVD, Grizzly Adams Productions, Inc., 2000.

10 Ian Wilson, Taped Interview, Behold a Mystery, Ariel Productions, Paul Bershon, Producer.

11 Kenneth Stevenson, Interview, *The Shroud of Turin: Is It the Burial Cloth of Jesus?* DVD, Grizzly Adams Productions, Inc., 2000.

12 Daniel Scavone, PhD, "The Scientific Shroud," *Mysteries of the Ancient World* (Banbury, CN: Dell Publishing, 1995), P. 98.

13 Russell Breault, "The Scientific Shroud," *Mysteries of the Ancient World* (Banbury, CN: Dell Publishing, 1995), P. 99.

14 Stevenson, *The Shroud of Turin.*

15 Mechthild Flury-Lemburg, Ph.D, *Sindone 2002,* (Torino: Editrea ODPF, 2003), P. 77-79.

16 Ibid. 8

17 Mechthild Flury-Lemburg, Ph.D, personal conversation with Joseph Meier of Grizzly Adams Productions, May 6, 2006, Turin, Italy.

ELEVEN

THE MYSTERY OF FRENCH WEAVING

In spite of comprehensive demonstrations by numerous scientific disciplines that show the limitations of Carbon-14 testing, and of all the scientific analyses that place the cloth in Jerusalem and Edessa in the first to third centuries, many critics and skeptics cling to the idea that the Carbon-14 testing alone makes the Shroud a medieval relic. But what if both sides are right? What if the Carbon-14 tests are as accurate as modern technology can make them, yet all of the other scientific data that places the cloth solidly in the first century is also accurate? That paradox has been raised, not by some obscure scientific analysis, but by the ancient art of historic research, and twenty-first century, space age science.

In 2005, a paper was presented at the Third International Dallas Shroud Conference, which suggested historic and scientific evidence indicating the carbon dating could be accurate on the samples tested, while at the same time asserting the possibility that all of the other scientific evidence of authenticity is also valid.

How could that be possible?

The Patch Theory

Several years earlier, Alan Adler had espoused the reweave theory. At the 2000 Symposium in Ovieto, Italy, authors M. Sue Benford and Joseph Marino presented a paper based on the premise that a sixteenth century "invisible patch" had skewed the 1988 Carbon-14 test on the sample from the Shroud of Turin. The idea was immediately refuted as being technically impossible. World-renowned textile expert, Mechthild Flury-Lemburg, who supervised the 2002 restoration of the Shroud, concluded in her book about that restoration that "reweaving in the literal sense does not exist."[1]

But is that true? Michael Erlich, president of Without a Trace, a company in Chicago, Illinois, claims to have provided invisible mending services for more than 20 years. According to Mr. Erlich:

Today, there is a modern, time-saving technique called "inweaving" that would be invisible from the surface, but easily recognizable from the back. However, the technique used in sixteenth century Europe called "French weaving" is an entirely different matter. French weaving involves a tedious thread-by-thread restoration that is, indeed, invisible. Sixteenth century owners of the Shroud certainly had enough material resources and weeks of time at their disposal to accomplish the task.[2]

What could have happened to an artifact under the direct protection of the Savoys, the ruling family of Italy, that would require them to put forth the time, effort, and money to accomplish such a thing? The short answer is "politics and promises."

Was such a repair within the capability of the sixteenth century master weavers? Campbell's answer is to the point, "The sixteenth century weavers were magicians."[3]

But even if it is possible, is it likely? Raymond Rogers, chemist at the Los Alamos National Laboratory and a member of the original STURP research team, didn't think so and set himself to the task of discovering whether or not scientific analysis could resolve the issue. Some years earlier, Rogers had been given a sample of the Shroud fabric by Gilbert Raes, the man who in 1973 had been charged with providing samples to those few scientists who had been invited to view the Shroud at that time. The sample had remained in his collection, unused, but he knew it came from the area of the Shroud immediately adjacent to the area from which the Carbon-14 samples had been taken. Rogers had also been given a portion of the retained "control" sample for comparison.

In a taped interview shortly before his death, Rogers expressed his initial skepticism, "This is just about the last straw, and I've got the sample that can shoot that full of holes," he said confidently, speaking of the historic research by Adler and later Benford and Marino. "I got out the Raes samples, and I got out the Shroud samples and went to work again, and lo and behold, in less than an hour I knew that [the] Raes sample here … radio carbon sample there, their warp threads and a few weft threads, they share for sure. I knew that the Raes sample was totally different in chemical composition than the main part of the Shroud. I had to believe it when the chemistry was different. And then the shocker that really shook me up. I hit this one that was an end-to-end splice, and it's exactly the sort of thing Benford and Marino were talking about in this invisible reweaving."[4]

A Rewoven Area

Ray Rogers' work with the Raes sample demonstrated that the Carbon-14 sample, which was cut from an area immediately adjacent to where the Raes sample was taken—was part of the rewoven area. And since it was cut from an area immediately adjacent to where the Carbon-14 sample was cut, the Carbon-14 sample was part of the rewoven area.

According to Tom D'Muhala, President of the American Shroud of Turin Association for Research (AMSTAR), the group that sponsored the 2005 Dallas Symposium, "It was on the portion of the Carbon-14 retain sample that Ray performed his defining work, which verified his hypothesis that the Raes and the Carbon-14 samples were both from a rewoven area, and not from the actual Shroud."[5]

Rogers died shortly after giving this interview, but before his death, he formalized his work in a paper, "Studies on the Radiocarbon Sample from the Shroud of Turin." Tom D'Muhala was granted permission to read Ray Rogers' paper at the 2005 Dallas Conference.[6]

According to D'Muhala, "Ray Rogers had expressed concerns over the results of the Carbon-14 test, due to the fact that the area from which the samples were cut fluoresced differently than the rest of the Shroud when excited with an ultra-violet source. Even though he was very skeptical of the Benford-Marino research, he knew he had in his possession the means to confirm or put to rest once and for all his own doubts and the claims made by the researchers. After completing his exhaustive tests, he wrote:

> The radiocarbon sampling area is uniquely coated with a yellow-brown plant gum containing dye lakes. Pyrolysis-mass-spectrometry results from the sample area, coupled with microscopic and microchemical observations, prove that the radiocarbon sample was NOT [emphasis added] part of the original cloth of the Shroud of Turin. The radiocarbon date was thus not valid for determining the true age of the Shroud.[7]

After reaching this conclusion, Rogers, in a telephone conversation with his longtime associate, said, "Tom, there is no scientific wriggle room."[8]

In addition, Dr. Whanger's studies on x-rays of the Shroud show conclusively that area of the sample had been altered and rewoven.

Another Carbon-14 Test?

Do these findings mean the scientific dilemma has been resolved? Hardly! When asked about Rogers' work and the seemingly irrefutable result, Mechthild Flury-Lemburg stated flatly, "There is no reweaving."[9] She maintains that since the French weavers had only the "naked eye" to work with, and their result would have to be visible to the naked eye.

But there was something else. Vernon Miller, the official STURP photographer, remembered that in 1978 those portions of the Shroud from which the Carbon-14 sample was taken, fluoresced differently than the main part of the Shroud, but at the time, this had seemed to be of only minimal interest. Now that a definite difference in those portions of the fabric had been scientifically proven, the fluorescence took on new significance.

The obvious resolution to this whole matter, of course, is to do another Carbon-14 test while adhering to the original protocols with samples being taken from different locations on the Shroud. But since the process of Carbon-14 testing involves the destruction of the sample, the Church has been reluctant to give up any more samples. Furthermore, if Flury-Lemburg's analysis of the carbon residue permeating the entire fabric is correct, the result would be the same regardless as to where on the cloth the sample was obtained. So while the science on both sides of the issue can perhaps be vindicated, the 1988 Carbon-14 test now appears to have been invalidated for the Shroud but accurate for the rewoven and patched sample area.

The search continues for evidence that might corroborate the authenticity of the Shroud. In John 20:6–7 we read:

> Then Simon Peter, who was behind him, arrived and went into the tomb. He saw the strips of linen lying there, as well as the burial cloth that had been around Jesus' head. The cloth was folded up by itself, separate from the linen (NIV).

The Bible clearly states that there were two pieces of cloth in the tomb. As discussed earlier, Dr. Mark Guscin has enumerated the findings of a number of scientists who have declared that a bloodstained linen cloth called the Sudarium of Oviedo is that second cloth. The documented history of this artifact goes back much further than the undisputed timeline of the Shroud. The implication, so far as the Shroud is concerned, is that if both cloths covered the same face and body, the 1988 Carbon-14 testing on the Shroud of Turin is further invalidated.

What is the truth about the Shroud? Hundreds of other tests have been carried out on the Shroud of Turin. All of them, with the exception of the largely discredited Carbon-14 test, give the Shroud of Turin a far greater claim to authenticity than any other ancient artifact, or for that matter, any other object on Earth.

But what about future scientific discoveries? Is there anything that connects the new discoveries to the old beliefs? Are there scientific secrets that can be gleaned from examining the cloth further? Are there secrets now coming to light in the scientific world that have been hidden in this stunning artifact for hundreds of years?

Science marches on, and precisely where it is headed, no one can be sure. One thing seems certain, however, and that is that the Shroud of Turin will remain an object of intense scrutiny by historians, theologians, and scientists until the mystery is solved.

But one more mystery hovers on the horizon. At least one scientist sees the Shroud, not so much as a mystery of the past, but as a clue to the very beginning of the universe.

That intriguing possibility is next.

Endnotes

1   Flury-Lemburg, Mechthild. *Sindone 2002*, (Torino: Editrea ODPF, 2003) P. 77-79.

2   Michael Erlich, Interview, *The Fabric of Time*, DVD, David W. Balsiger, Senior Producer, Grizzly Adams Productions, Inc., 2006.

3   Ibid.

4   Ray Rogers, "In His Own Words," presented at the Dallas Shroud Symposium, 2005. Ray Roger's paper was published by Elsevier B.V. in Thermochimica Acta (2005), P. 189-194, <http://www.elsevier.com/locate/tca>

5   Tom D'Muhala, Letter to Grizzly Adams Staff, *The Fabric of Time*, DVD, David W. Balsiger, Senior Producer, Grizzly Adams Productions, Inc., 2006.

6   Rogers.

7   Studies on the radiocarbon sample from the Shroud of Turin, Raymond N. Rogers, 2005.

8   Tom D'Muhala, *The Fabric of Time*.

9   Mechthild Flury Lemburg, P. 77-79.

Twelve

DISCOVERY OF A NEW PHYSICS

Up to this point, the study of the Shroud had taken one direction—scientists and historians used known tests to determine facts about the Shroud. They all assumed that known physical processes had created the image on the cloth. Then something extraordinary happened. Scientists began to question the usefulness of applying tests for known processes to something that was out of the realm of physics—the Resurrection. If the image is truly a record of the Resurrection of Jesus Christ, the *process* of such an event is unknown. Christ's Resurrection was a one-time, unique event, not duplicated since. Therefore how can it be tested? What would we look for? This was the dilemma facing scientists in the new millennium.

Today we live in a world of scientific information unheard of just a few years ago. The discovery of the DNA strand, coupled with the amazing capacity of computers, has made it possible to map the entire human genome. The Hubble telescope lets us look to and explore deeper regions of our solar system. We are able to witness these images as satellites skip past unknown worlds, while huge radio antennas listen for even the tiniest whisper from the very center of space. Recently, astronomers even declared they have detected the first split-second of the universe. New theories about the nature of information and matter are being formulated at this moment.

According to Dr. William Wolkowski, Professor of Physics at P.M. Curie University of Paris, "the essence of physical law is information."[1] One of the universal, modern axioms of creation is: "Information cannot be changed because then it becomes 'other' information."

Dame Isabel Piczek, who, in addition to being a monumental artist is also a particle physicist with an international reputation, recently made some statements regarding the nature of information and matter.

All physical laws and consequently all formation of matter is created and animated by the single, particular, well-defined essence of the information penetrating them through and through. When science finds discrepancies in matter or phenomenon behaving differently from its own usual law, it is the doubtless signal of new, unknown information, not a changing of the original information that has to remain the same.

These "discrepancies" are more easily detected regarding the micro world, but more recently we are learning to notice them also in the macro world. One can ultimately say: The universe is made of information and its resonance.[2]

Intelligent Energy

Science tells us that we are bathed in a field of intelligent energy. Scientists, even though they don't know exactly what it means, acknowledge the existence of this field, and they have even discovered that the DNA within our body communicates directly with this energy. Dr. Edgar Mitchell, a former astronaut, the sixth man to walk on the moon and founder of Noetic Sciences, along with several colleagues, developed a model that just may bring us closer to understanding what this means. According to Dr. Mitchell, "The universe that this model leads us to is an intelligent, self-organizing, creative, learning, trial-and-error, participatory, interactive, non-locally interconnected evolutionary system. That's what it's all about."[3]

But how do these new and exciting things that physicists have discovered fit into an investigation of the Shroud of Turin? In a personal interview in 2006, Dr. Mitchell brought these findings to date: "It's been known for a long time that all matter emits and reabsorbs particle energy. Over a hundred years ago, Max Planck named these emissions 'Quanta,' and they have been the study of particle physics for over a hundred years. If you analyze all the emissions from any physical object ... that's called a quantum hologram. And what we now know that we didn't know before is that every object is a quantum object!"[4]

The basic ideas behind relativity and quantum physics are comprehensible. The essence of relativity is summed up in a single, concise sentence: *The laws of physics are the same for all observers in uniform motion.*

The study of physics has produced a set of laws that scientists call The Standard Model. It is one of the most profound and powerful products of human understanding. This is the theory that summarizes the scientists' current understanding of elementary particles and the fundamental forces of nature. These theories sum up all the physical laws we live by.

But there are some things the standard model doesn't address. For example, Dr. William Wolkowski has suggested that the Shroud, as a case of physical archaeology, "offers the possibility of selecting a cosmology compatible with such macroscopic dematerialization (MDM) and reversible macroscopic teleportation (RMT)."[5] *In other words, when Jesus was raised from the dead, he transcended the usual laws of matter and motion, going into another world from this world.* This contradicts the physical laws by which we are bound. This does not fit into the Standard Model.

If we can deal with unknown information creating its own world system, as Professor Wolkowski, Dr. Mitchell, and Dame Piczek suggest, does that mean the physical world as we have come to know it may in fact be different than we think it is? Dame Piczek makes some startling suggestions:

Let me apologize in advance for making such daring statements, but I think some of the greatest geniuses in the world of physics have caused the greatest puzzles. Einstein's "space-time," neither of which are really known, appear to be equal in impact and power. The Uncertainty Principle puts a big dent in that. In truth, *Time* very much has the upper hand. Our world is obviously Space Trapped in Time. Everything moves with uncertain reality captured in the constantly changing speed limit of time. The Other World, the sister world, is Time Trapped in Space. In that world system, there is no need for movement. All things are real, and everything exists everywhere at once.[6]

What would it be like to live in a dimension where *Time* doesn't rule? Where we don't have to think in terms of *past, present and future.* We can't even imagine a world like that. But that's exactly where the Resurrection leads.

Could it be that the quantum "revolution" in physics permits science to go beyond human speculation? According to one quantum physicist—the world is even more extraordinary than we thought.

Are there two worlds, *space trapped in time,* and *time trapped in space?* And are they actually interchangeable? Where would we begin to look for a meaningful example of what all of this means to you and me? Is it just some cosmic Rubric's Cube for scientists to play with, or is it possible that there is a broader purpose—ancient information perhaps—that is even more relevant today? And where does the Resurrection fit into these proposed theories of physics and the nature of the world?

The Shroud May Hold the Key

Oddly enough, it is the ordinary piece of cloth that we have been discussing that gives science its most tangible clues. Dame Isabel Piczek has presented an important paper that suggests there is new information based upon data derived from the Shroud that could answer the secret of what happened to the body of Christ at the very moment of the Resurrection. According to Dame Piczek, it is a question worth pursuing. "I think the Resurrection of Christ, as a miracle and as a spiritual phenomenon, should be left to theology to discuss. But the bodily Resurrection, the Shroud of Turin, and the whole circumstance of the image on the Shroud, involves matter, although matter seen in a startlingly different way. And I believe it is essential that we try to find the extraordinary laws of matter that exist within the Shroud image."[7]

In an extremely significant paper presented at the 2005 Shroud Conference in Dallas, Texas, Dame Piczek went beyond dealing with the position of the body within the cloth and brought attention to an undiscovered *interface*. This mysterious interface divides the image transport into two hermetically separate, though simultaneous, actions, and forces the Shroud linen to be taut and parallel on both sides. In other words, the upper part of the cloth (that was over the body of Christ) and the lower part of the cloth (that was under the body of Christ) were both stretched tight at the moment of the image-forming event. This discovery brought out another completely overlooked factor of the Shroud image—that the two images on the Shroud are also semi-three-dimensional, very much like a bas relief. Accordingly, they record the side image in two halves in a most complex way. In other words, it's as if the image were imprinted on both sides of the cloth simultaneously, as if both sides at the same time recorded each curve of the body. This bas relief effect cannot be fully explained even by modern science.[8]

Shroud Leads to New Physical Laws

What follows is a summary of Dame Piczek's findings, taken directly from her notes from the 2005 International Dallas Conference on the Shroud of Turin paper, and reproduced here with her permission.

Perhaps we have built up for ourselves a commonplace, manmade world, the result of human speculation that does not exist. The Quantum Revolution was the first that was not really created by men; we accidentally stumbled into it. Some quantum physicists have pointed out that anyone who claims to understand quantum physics does not understand it. In any case, it is absolutely valid to try to find the extraordinary laws of matter that exist in connection with the Shroud image. Indeed, the Shroud must lead to the formulation of new physical laws. Some of the existing laws we believe in will have to be dropped altogether; they are nonexistent. Others will have to be changed, and still others refined. The fact is, we live mostly in a world of false reality.

In the common world, it is universally believed that we sit on solid chairs, drive cars made from solid materials, our surroundings supposedly filled with sound. In reality, we sit mostly on vacuum, drive vacuum, we ourselves are mostly vacuum, and the sound around us is mostly silence. How do we even start to get closer to the truth of creation?

Most academic physicists would radically exclude any mention of the Shroud as something out of which any science, and especially a new science, could arise, except perhaps for some antiquated tests on the sheer physical entity of the old linen itself. That philosophy didn't take us very far even in Shroud research proper.

Let us try to turn this around. Maybe we will get somewhere.[9]

In other words, let's not approach the Shroud with the scientific principles we count on in this world, but look at the Shroud as representing forces that we don't know anything about.

Beyond the Laws of Nature

Dame Piczek's point is that *the image on the Shroud cannot and will not adhere to the physical laws of our world as we know it.*

Where can you find a scientific law that can explain the Resurrection? There isn't one. It can't. So perhaps we should be looking at the Shroud from the context of a whole new paradigm—one of trying to determine what the image is and how it came to be—on its own terms—not on ours. Dame Piczek continues:

If this Shroud is truly the Shroud of Christ, with his image formulated on it, there is one obvious certainty; whatever the physical process of the Resurrection and the consequent image formation, absolutely no change could or should have taken place in the body of Christ. That body must have passed from one world system to the other unchanged, leaving nothing behind except already detached blood; gaining nothing nor changing into anything that was not already in its makeup and capacity.

While all of that may not be within our present grasp, it actually should be a starting point for the new physics. An extraordinary law is hidden in its depth, the law of *interchangeableness*, (meaning from one world system into the other). The Shroud is a sheer demonstration of this. At the moment, we have not mastered even a marginal understanding of this, but we have to take the first step on the road to what could be the greatest human advancement in physics, cosmology, and the key to the real nature of intelligent existence. The great question that remains is: What is it that keeps this side of creation from readily submitting to the law of interchangeableness? What is the barrier that prevents this world system from changing into the other and back? Is there some sign of it in the subatomic world? So far, it seems the only such exchange happened with the physical body of Christ, so we may assume that the body of Christ must have passed from one world system to the other, unchanged, and leaving nothing behind. The difference is in power; a power that the body always had, but a power that within the new world system no thing interferes with.[10]

Jesus Is Creator and Sustainer

Quoted again is a verse from the preface that explains how Christ is holding all of creation together: "For by him all things were created: things in heaven and on earth, visible and invisible, whether thrones or powers or rulers or authorities; all things were created by him and for him. He is before all things, and in him all things hold together." (Col. 1:16, 17, NIV).

Accordingly, Jesus is not only the creator of the world, but he also keeps it "running." He is the Sustainer. Through him, everything is held together, protected, and prevented from disintegrating into chaos. As the one who made the physical laws and maintains those laws, he is above the physical laws and the confines of time in our world. With his Resurrection, however, he superseded the physical laws of this world. Dame Piczek explains:

> The total lack of success over the years by those attempting to duplicate the image formation might be due to the fact that in every instance the unchangeable character of the body of Christ was disrespected. Each method tried to employ known and destructive processes. The proton and later the neutron flux theory, the assistance of free radicals, a nuclear transformation affecting the body ¼ inch deep, total body disintegration and the Shroud falling through it, etc.; all of these suggestions involve a change in the body. All suggest destructive changes much greater than the breaking of the legs or putrefaction. In all

of these, the integrity of the body would have been lowered far below anything compatible with Resurrection. (I realize that the Resurrection is not something physics discusses, but if this is the Shroud of Christ, the Resurrection still has to be the reference point that measures the accuracy or feasibility of a suggestion.)[11]

Nothing Was Left Behind

When Christ appeared after his Resurrection, his body was intact. Nothing had been left behind, as shown in the Shroud. Luke 24:36-43 (NIV) describes the scene days after the Resurrection:

> While they [the disciples] were still speaking, Jesus himself stood among them and said to them, "Peace be with you." They were startled and frightened, thinking they saw a ghost. He said to them, "Why are you troubled, and why do doubts rise in your minds? Look at my hands and my feet. It is I myself! Touch me and see; a ghost does not have flesh and bones, as you see I have." When he had said this he showed them his hands and feet. And while they still did not believe it because of joy and amazement, he asked them, Do you have anything here to

eat? They gave him a piece of a broiled fish, and he took it and ate it in their presence (NIV).

The only thing left behind during the Resurrection was the blood that had welled out of his body before his body was buried. On the cloth is the record of how the body was changed into the other world system. Dame Piczek goes on to formulate even more:

> The hope for a solution that maintains the integrity of the body of Christ and opens new doors presented itself when the existence of a new entity, the *Interface-Event Horizon* of the Shroud, and one of its visible byproducts, the bas-relief effect, was found and partially defined by sculptural illustrations. Partially because the Interface-Event Horizon is the most complex entity with which one can be faced, the old physics does not solve any of its extraordinary properties.

This is where the problem of solving the riddle of the newly discovered Entity, the Interface Event Horizon, arises. It is not just a problem of Shroud research, but of physics, cosmology, and as you might expect, the anthropic principle as well. *The Shroud is truly the gate of the future.*

Because of the projected law of interchangeableness between the two world systems, we must be prepared to rethink what we know about science. Even though the physical laws we thought to be valid will have to be adjusted, when the Shroud is used as the reference point, these laws still cast some light on the path of research. For starters, if the image formation (when the image was imprinted on the cloth) happened through the assistance of the Interface-Event Horizon (when the laws of physics are changed in some way) and not through something being taken away from the wholeness and unchanged integrity of the body (Jesus' body was intact, unchanged), then the elements to study become:

1) An instantaneous action at a distance.

2) The structure and nature of fields; an unknown, new field and its action, most probably the information field.

3) The Absolute Zero collapse of time. (The Time quantum velocity drops to Absolute Zero.)

4) The physics of an Event Horizon. (In general relativity, we have found that there

are certain things called "black holes." The surface of a black hole is called an Event Horizon ... and it's called that because right at that surface ... the laws of physics seem to change character drastically.) [See Notes: The Event Horizon of the Shroud under the footnotes at the end of this chapter.]

The existence of the image on the Shroud proves the Zero Collapse of the Time Quantum and vice versa; the collapse of the Time Quantum necessitates the image. Absolute Zero, however, does not exist in nature. What happened in the tomb of Christ is a unique, singular event when Absolute Zero was achieved.

When Christ was resurrected, he did so outside the parameters of time. He went from one world system to the other in a shorter time period than the "blink of an eye." This is not something that the laws of physics can explain. The hold that time has on our creation was shattered by Jesus in his Resurrection, and that is something that we cannot duplicate. His Resurrection happened in "Absolute Zero" time. Dame Pizcek explains:

Although the zero collapse of time is not the only description of the action of the Interface Event Horizon, it is one of the important ones. As a partial conclusion: The creation of the image as a visual Entity was seemingly assisted by the collapse of Quantum Time velocity to Absolute Zero, its physics and chemistry simply standing in the next phase in a different world system. No one could cause a phase transition in the nature of the collapse of Time Quantum. That's why there is only one Shroud of Turin.[12]

For most of us trying to absorb the full meaning of the quantum theories suggested here, the theories will simply be beyond our capability to fully comprehend. We can be certain, however, that the image on the Shroud exists, and so far it has defied all means of explaining or duplicating it by any other means. What is gratifying for those seriously searching for the truth is that the scientists and the men and women of faith are beginning to reach out to one another in anticipation that the answers will be both intellectually satisfying and spiritually satisfying. Both are acknowledging that the Resurrection of Christ was an event far beyond anything we have ever seen before. Both agree that the Resurrection is the event that can change the world—not only the spiritual world, but also the scientific world.

Is Isabel Piczek out on a limb of physics where no one else wants to go? The next chapter will investigate another promising area of discovery—quantum holograms.

Endnotes

1   Dr. William Wolkowski, Professor of Physics at P.M. Curie University of Paris, Written statement to Grizzly Adams staff, Dec. 30, 2005.

2   Dame Isabel Piczek. Notes on the 3rd International Dallas Conference on the Shroud of Turin 2005 Symposium Paper.

3   Dr. Edgar Mitchell, Interview, *The Fabric of Time*, DVD. David W. Balsiger, Senior Producer, Grizzly Adams Productions, Inc., 2006.

4   Ibid.

5   Wolkowski.

6   Piczek.

7   Ibid.

8   Ibid.

9   Ibid.

10 Ibid.

11 Ibid.
12 Dame Isabel Piczek. Notes on the 3rd International Dallas Conference on the Shroud of Turin 2005 Symposium Paper.

Notes: The Event Horizon of the Shroud

[Taken from Dame Isabel Piczek, May 2007 notes regarding the Interface Event Horizon]:

The image on the Shroud is the trail of powerful changes in forces even on a cosmological scale. These forces established themselves, then afterward they were forcibly cancelled. They either left their visible traces on the Shroud, or the trace that is left necessitates the existence of a previous condition, through which that necessity establishes its undeniable presence. These events, visibly recorded on the Shroud, followed each other in an infinitely small time scale. One has to know the physical phenomena to recognize the traces they left and their sequences. The image actually is filled with movement.

We have stated there is a dividing line, a real **interface** between the projection of the Frontal Image and the Dorsal Image that was, no doubt, created by the body wrapped into the Shroud.

Revealing Signs

The following signs indicate that the Shroud was forced absolutely taut and precisely parallel with some kind of horizontal entity running in the center. Also apparent is the presence of an inner Enclosure, an *Isolated System*, with all that this Isolated System would indicate or even enforce:

a. The hermetic separation of the two images, Frontal and Dorsal, without any overlap.

b. The lack of anatomical distortion of the naked Body projected on the Shroud.

c. It is clearly visible on the Shroud images, especially on the Dorsal image, that the muscles of the Body are not crushed and flattened against the stone bench of the tomb.

d. The Body is hovering between the upper and lower sheet, and there is *no trace of gravity.*

e. The lack of gravity is also further proven by the Shroud linen. The linen does not fall on top of the Body, but remains in its unnaturally stretched condition at some distance from the Body.

All the above tell us that the Interface indicated is not an ordinary Interface. Judging by its qualities, it has to be an Event Horizon that blocks every communication between the two sides of the image. This statement, however, in spite of the visible traces of an Interface Event Horizon on the Shroud, has to be thoroughly investigated. No doubt there are some powerful paradoxes involved here signaling either new laws, or laws that were not recognized before, or an altogether new world system.

Event Horizon Defined

Let us see what is usually indicated by an Event Horizon and how this relates to the Event Horizon of the Shroud, if at all?

An Event Horizon is a critical line or a radius that divides Spacetime into two distinct regions. The exterior region one can experience, but the region beyond the critical line or radius one cannot experience. The critical line marks the path of the last light pulse that reached the Event Horizon and Time itself slowed to a halt. Looking at the critical line from the other side of Time when events gain almost infinite speed, one could see the full history of the Universe, past, present, and future rapidly passing toward an arbitrary end.

Ordinarily, Event Horizons are tied to gravity and time, until both, Time and Space, cease to exist in a Black Hole, and the end product of the process and gravity suffer a catastrophic collapse.

Does the Interface Event Horizon of the Shroud lead to a Black Hole? Everything on the Shroud indicates that the answer is *no.* It is here that we face the most substantial paradox of our investigation. A paradox of that magnitude one cannot solve all at once, but one can assemble everything that is known so far, and get closer to the magic door or opening through the Shroud, into a startlingly different world.

We have stated before that the Images on the Shroud firmly indicate the total absence of gravity. Yet they also firmly indicate the presence of an Event Horizon. How? These two facts seemingly contradict each other.

These two firmly established traces on the Shroud—the absence of gravity and the presence of an Event Horizon—necessitate the past presence of something more powerful than gravity, which had the capacity to solve the above paradox.

Entropy Turned Around

Einstein hypothesized that Pressure, Stress, and Energy can add to gravity. His followers, continuing this exercise, concluded that if these were administered in sufficiently powerful doses, gravity could be overpowered. (One of the suggestions was negative gravity, but I am not talking here about negative gravity.)

Decreasing entropy can produce energy levels powerful enough to replace gravity while leaving other gravity-like effects in place, as the Event Horizon. This has to be further studied. It promises some novel results.

The upper region of the Isolated System of the Shroud has one Event Horizon, H1, that serves as a boundary of the Upper Region, and there has to be an Event Horizon, H2, that is boundary to the Lower Region of the closed system. There is no space region but infinite density between the two. The two boundaries can be looked at as one. Because H1 and H2 move so close to each other, they look as one. It makes them eventually disappear, causing a total collapse of the Time Quantum to Absolute Zero Time.

The total Space and Time breakdown to zero exposes what was in the heart of the now collapsed Event Horizon—not a black hole, but a very special kind of Singularity, similar to the one that once assisted the creation of a universe—our universe.

THIRTEEN

HOLOGRAPHIC IMAGE
DISCOVERIES

Science has entered territories not dreamed of even a year or two ago. As scientists have received more information from deeper regions of space, and as technology has advanced to go deeper into the tiniest parts of creation, old ideas about the universe have been challenged.

Physics professor Fred Allen Wolf states, "Physicists have achieved a lot of success, and we think that we have pretty much everything, but it turns out we know we don't. We know there are missing links. We know there are puzzles cropping up all the time. And believe me, people are working to find the answers."[1]

If anything touches infinity, it's the Shroud of Christ. But how can scientists find the answer to the information the Shroud contains? Dr. Edgar Mitchell and a group of scientists trying to identify things that are fundamental to the way nature works made some startling discoveries.

> The classical traditional model of physics, which began in Newtonian times, describes how particles and atoms and molecules move and recombine. Even most of the twenty-first century physicists only look at the particle aspects of it and really don't concentrate very much on the informational aspect. And it's only, really, with the Quantum Hologram that we have brought information up to a par of importance with energy itself and with physicality so that we understand that the universe we live in not only exists because of its physicality, but it's understood because of its information. And this is a powerful new concept. And all physical bodies have these holographic emissions that are available non-locally, which means throughout the universe ... non-locally at all times.[2]

Science is now acknowledging that the transfer of information is one of the vital activities of all matter. For example, our DNA records millions of bits of information that makes it possible for you to be uniquely you. All matter can give us vital information. A quantum hologram is part of this knowledge.

Quantum Hologram

What is a quantum hologram? "The quantum hologram," Dr. Mitchell explains, "is merely a method of describing the emissions, total emissions from an object, very much like if you look at your fingertip, at the little swirls on your fingertip. It doesn't tell you very much about you, but if you look at the swirls on all ten fingers all at once, that's your fingerprints, and it uniquely defines you and identifies you. The emissions from a physical object, when studied as a whole, uniquely identify events in the history of that object."[3]

Through a quantum hologram, we supposedly can get a picture of the entire subject just by looking at the emissions from information generated by any part of it. Like ripples on water from the dropping of stones into its depth, information is generated that divulges information about the incident.

The theory of quantum holograms has generated much more research on the Shroud. Dr. Petrus Soons, working with a group of scientists in Eindhoven, Holland, is preparing an experiment that utilizes the three-dimensional information encoded in the Shroud image in a completely different way.

Along with Tom D'Muhala, Dr. Soons wants to examine a single fibril taken from an image area, to determine if holographic information resides in the Shroud itself. If so, a hologram of the entire image can be recreated. Much like DNA, in a true hologram, information about the whole image is contained in every part of the image. Their pursuit is to unlock the door to this treasure-trove of data. This is important because some of the information, such as a picture of the arms on the image where the fire destroyed the image, is missing.

Some scientists believe the characteristics of the image on the Shroud—such as three-dimensional information from a two-dimensional photograph, the negative aspect of the image, and the fact that the front and back images that appear on the cloth are virtually free of distortion—are basically holographic. Is this where the Shroud image and quantum physics finally connect? Or is there something even beyond the quantum hologram?

Viewing it as merely an object, what events in the history of the Shroud might we expect to find? According to Professor Wolkowski, the new concepts and questions that arise from this study of the Shroud are:

1) Why was the enshrouded body subject to MDM/RMT (macroscopic dematerialization—MDM—and reversible macroscopic teleportation—RMT)? Was this an informational strategy related to yet unknown informational symmetry laws? (These concepts are defined later in the book.)

2) What was the mechanism of the MDM/RMT?

3) If and where did it rematerialize?

4) Was the body composed of different matter, incompatible with that of earthly or intergalactic matter? and

5) What was the informational (phoronic) description of this matter?

The retrospective, (nearly forensic) description of this informational strategy, even if related to a case of state-specific-science, may lead to the formulation of new physical laws, a refinement of existing ones and support for a reinforced anthropic principle.[4]

From a layperson's point of view, this means that we can gain new information about our world from examining the image because it contains information about an event that transcends our physical laws. When Christ's body went from one world to another, the record of that event was embedded in the Shroud's image. What can we learn about our world—how it was created, and how the physical laws work—from examining the image?

Investigating Hologram Images

In 1931, Giuseppe Enrie, a professional photographer, was commissioned to make a photographic record of the Shroud in connection with a royal event, the marriage of the Prince of Savoy, a great many photographs were taken. Enrie used much more sophisticated equipment than Seconda Pia had used back in the nineteenth century. Enrie's photographs were of much better quality than Pia's. At the same time, Enrie's photographs were taken at a period of time when cameras still had to use time-lapse photography to create their images. Consequently, because of the longer exposure time required, cameras of Enrie's day often recorded more detail than do modern cameras which take photographs in an instant.

Dr. Petrus Soons reasoned that if the negatives of Enrie's photographs contained the three-dimensional information known to be contained in the Shroud image, a full hologram of the image may be possible. He took the negatives to the Eindhoven Holographic Laboratory in Holland near Amsterdam to see if the experts would be willing to test his theory. His ideas were not enthusiastically received.

> When I came in there with my photographs and told them there was 3-D information, they were very skeptical about it because normally you don't make a hologram of a photograph. Then they started experimenting, and they found out they could make a hologram from this material.

> It is very important to note also that we didn't change any data, so all the information that is in the digitized files is also in the hologram. What we did in the laboratory is we checked the whole Shroud for existing 3-D information. The only 3-D information we found was in the image of the body. The

whole body hologram gave us the possibility to see the image of the man on the Shroud under angles that have never been seen before.

We could confirm a couple of the findings, for example, the round objects on the eyes … we cannot see inscriptions, but we can confirm that they are solid metal objects. A point of controversy has always been the position of the legs because you cannot see that very well on the photograph. On the hologram, it shows extraordinary well. The left leg was stretched. The foot was put in a diagonal position fixed to the cross. That's why the leg is [bent]. [The soldiers] used one nail to nail both feet and fix them to the cross.[5]

The astounding fact was that the other items pictured on the cloth (the flowers, pollen, etc.) did not form a hologram, or show up on the hologram. Only the body did.

The Amulet
The hologram provided yet another exciting surprise for Dr. Soons and his associates, but on which additional research needs to be done:

The most exciting thing we found in the hologram was under the beard. It was known already that there was a wide line, but nobody could ever say what that exactly meant or what it was. It is a solid object. It is in a form something like an amulet that was put there. Now after studying it for quite a while, I could figure out that there were letters on it, on top, slightly raised."[6]

The holographic information is beginning to reach further into the information realm than anyone thought possible. Dr. Gary Habermas, a distinguished Professor and Chair of the Department of Philosophy and Theology at Liberty University, finds the discovery not only fascinating, but timely as well.

This information is going to have to be checked out, but if it were confirmed, this would just be along the lines of several other things that have been written just recently, I mean hot off the press books, which are saying in early Christianity, two messages were preached from the very beginning: Jesus is divine and he was raised from the dead. Those two are right there at the beginning. They didn't come decades later. And of course, that's the same proclamation that we find in the Gospels and in [Paul's writings].[7]

Tom D'Muhala, who examined the hologram closely, was surprised by this development since the object wasn't visible on all of the photographs. He explained:

It turns out that the structure of the plaque is evident in some photographs and not in others, and the folks at the Dutch Holographic Laboratory in Eindhoven, Holland, found that slight variations in focusing distance, depth of field, brought the new [discovery] out. So on one photograph where this structure is evident, it was captured on film by pure luck. And that is suggestive that there may be a different structure visible at different depths in this image.[8]

Several Questions Cleared Up

The hologram clears up several questions that have long puzzled Shroud researchers. In addition to the question of the position of the legs discussed earlier, there has been an ongoing discussion about the position of the feet. Some historical descriptions of the position of the feet on the Shroud place the anatomical left foot on top of the right. According to Tom D'Muhala, the holograms show this is clearly not the case:

> On the evening of September 10, 2006, Isabel Piczek and I were examining the full-body, frontal and dorsal, holographic images of the Shroud of Turin, while Michael Minor, Donna D'Muhala, and Larry Vrzalik looked on. The holograms were of the negative images, just as they appear on the actual Shroud, with the wound in the side on the left.

Remember that the image on the Shroud is both frontal and dorsal, is on the side of the cloth that faced the body, and is a "mirror" image of the actual body. That is why it is necessary to indicate individual features as the "anatomical" left or "anatomical" right. Tom D'Muhala continues his observation:

> While examining the dorsal [back] image, Isabel noted that there was something peculiar about the legs and feet that seemed anatomically incorrect. As an example, the large toe, which was clearly visible on one of the feet, appeared to be on the wrong side of that foot. On closer examination, I saw

that the large toe was clearly and distinctly positioned as it naturally should be, but on the opposite foot. There is no mistake about the position of the feet. The anatomical right foot, which appears as the most well-defined foot on conventional 2D photographs of the Shroud, is placed *over* the left foot."

Before discovering that there is 3D information encoded in the Shroud image, some believed that the anatomical left foot lay on top of the right foot, but this is clearly not so.[9]

The Helmet of Thorns

Less well-known, but still a bone of contention among the experts, has been the long-accepted "crown of thorns" that encircled the head of the crucified Christ. Some have suggested that rather than a "crown," it was a "helmet" of thorns. According to Dr. Soons, the hologram resolves that issue as well.

On the original Shroud and the photographs, one can see a bloodspot that seems to be floating above the head. The hologram shows that this bloodspot is *on top* of the head due to a wound caused by a helmet of thorns. It basically confirms that there was a helmet of thorns and not a crown.[10]

The hologram does bring out in explicit detail what for centuries was hidden beneath the faint, barely visible markings on a piece of hand-woven linen fabric.

How Much Information?

While examining the hologram up close, Tom D'Muhala suggested to Dr. Soons that a *single fibril* from the Shroud image area may possibly be sufficient for determining whether the *entire image* contains holographic information. In that case, could the Shroud image itself be a hologram?

"And that's important for the Shroud of Turin," Dr. Soons tells us, "because the upper arms are missing because of a fire in 1532. So what I believe is that there is holographic information in the Shroud, which would make it possible to see the whole body of man of the Shroud … including the [missing] shoulders and upper arms."[11]

Dr. Soons is confident that holographic information is resident in the actual Shroud. Perhaps in the not too distant future, scientists may be able to create a full unblemished hologram of the entire image by examining a very small portion of the Shroud.

After having had a chance to examine the hologram, we asked both Dr. Alan Whanger and Tom D'Muhala to tell us if there is anything they had not seen before and to give us their impressions of the new data. Alan Whanger, who is a medical doctor, focused on the clarity of the physical features and the other objects he has so carefully studied over the years. "The hologram does a remarkable job of emphasizing certain features on the Shroud; it gives science a three-dimensional aspect to this and makes some of the features much more prominent. Particularly, the scourge marks that we see on the back are astonishingly revealed in the hologram. Also, we see certain parts of the body ... the toes ... some of the hair ... and actually one of the elbows on the hologram, which are not really that apparent on the regular photograph."[12]

Tom D'Muhala found a great deal to be excited about in these new holographic images. As an example, the discovery of the plaque around the neck is particularly significant.

"There are other things as well. For example, you can clearly see there is no distortion of the dorsal or backside image. These facts seem to support Isabel Piczek's hypothesis of a True Event Horizon. Had the body been lying on rock when the image was formed, distortion would have been unavoidable."[13]

Normally, when a body lies on a hard surface like a rock slab, the hard surface distorts the softer one (the flesh). But in the image on the Shroud, there is no distortion of the flesh (i.e., the buttocks and other features were not flattened in apperance). The body is formed perfectly without any dents or flattening or other changes that a hard surface would make on it.

D'Muhala goes on to give a summation of the nature of the Shroud:

> There are several aspects of the Shroud that aren't discussed very much. The most obvious is, it is still here; that it has survived through fire, flood, and the ravages of time. And even though it has presented the faithful and scientists alike with considerable challenges, it still has a message for all mankind. The more we work with it, the more we discover, and the more we come to realize that this could be a record of the literal Resurrection of Jesus Christ.[14]

Dr. Whanger made an affirmative statement about the importance of the Shroud and the feelings of those involved in studying it:

> The Shroud is the most astonishing object in existence, and certainly the most intensely studied, and the one that has the most important information for us human beings. We have no question that this is Jesus of Nazareth, and we believe that the event which occurred approximately 30 to 36 hours after death, with the body disappearing from the folded Shroud, indicates some unique event, which we call the Resurrection, had taken place. [This is] probably the most pivotal event in history, which is exemplified and witnessed by the Shroud.[15]

But the Shroud is not just a fascinating bit of history. It is a witness to the one event that defines history—and gives us hope. That is what we will discuss in our final chapter.

Endnotes

1   Dr. Fred Allen Wolf, Interview, *The Fabric of Time*, DVD, David W. Balsiger, Senior Producer, Grizzly Adams Productions, Inc., 2006.

2   Dr. Edgar Mitchell, Interview, *The Fabric of Time*, DVD, David W. Balsiger, Senior Producer, Grizzly Adams Productions, Inc., 2006.

3   Ibid.

4   Dr. William Wolkowski, Professor of Physics at P.M. Curie University of Paris, Written statement to Grizzly Adams staff, Dec. 30, 2005.

5   Dr. Petrus Soons, Interview, *The Fabric of Time*, DVD, David W Balsiger, Senior Producer, Grizzly Adams Productions, Inc., 2006.

6   Ibid.

7   Dr. Gary Habermas, Interview, *The Fabric of Time*, DVD, David W Balsiger, Senior Producer, Grizzly Adams Productions, Inc., 2006.

8   Tom D'Muhala, Interview, *The Fabric of Time*, DVD, David W Balsiger, Senior Producer, Grizzly Adams Productions, Inc., 2006.

9   Ibid.

10 Soons.

11 Ibid.

12 Dr. Alan Whanger, Interview, *The Fabric of Time*, DVD, David W Balsiger, Senior Producer, Grizzly Adams Productions, Inc., 2006.

13 Ibid.

14 D'Muhala.

15 Whanger.

FOURTEEN

IS THE CASE CLOSED?

A t this point, what does the Shroud of Turin mean to you? And even more importantly, what does the Resurrection of Christ mean to your life? The answers to these questions are vital.

Peter Schumacher, who described himself as a worldly man before his encounter with the Shroud of Turin, concluded his presentation at the 1998 First Dallas Shroud of Turin International Conference with a personal affirmation. He pointed his thumb back over his shoulder indicating the life-size photograph of the Shroud behind him and said, "I don't know about you, but that's my Savior."

These comments reflect the change that often comes over people who have encountered the Shroud in a personal way. It would appear that regardless of the scientific, archaeological, or theological determinations, many people have come to their own conclusions about the Shroud—what it is and where it came from. Given the fact that people who come into direct contact with this artifact invariably take away a renewed hope in the Resurrection of Jesus, it is unlikely that Carbon-14 tests, or polarized light microscopes, or any of the other 92 scientific tests will do much to change their conclusions.

The Question Posed

How do you answer the question: Is the Shroud of Turin the burial cloth of Jesus Christ? Many scientists are prepared to state that the case has been proven as well as anything can be proven. The work currently being done by Dr. Isabel Piczek, Dr. Petrus Soons, and Dr. Edgar Mitchell indicates that scientists are far from throwing in the towel in their search for definitive answers. And the search for answers from an ancient cloth is leading to even more exciting avenues of discovery. According to Dr. Mitchell, each step forward opens a new door of understanding. He explains:

Until modern times, science has not looked upon the subjective experience, but this quantum holographic development and understanding is changing all of that; it helps us get a handle on how information is utilized, something we've never had before.

The quantum hologram is now a real-time, ongoing phenomenon of emissions that carries information about physical objects including at death. Matter in the body continues to create history.[1]

It is possible that in discovering the answers to the questions posed by the Shroud we might also discover the greatest secrets of creation and life in the universe. Not only is this possibility intriguing, it has given the scientific world an entirely new quantum paradigm to contemplate. This astonishing artifact, in fact, has brought to light a whole new world of scientific and religious possibilities of understanding.

Like Mary Magdalene and the other women who were the first to arrive and discover the tomb empty, we also will find the tomb empty. But we have in our possession an ancient burial cloth with an image that bears witness to a tortured, crucified man. As we've seen, the image cannot be explained by any of the most advanced scientific analyses. But the definitive facts are outlined as follows:

1. The history of the Shroud can reasonably be traced back to the first century.

2. The flowers and the pollen on the Shroud prove the cloth has been in or near Jerusalem.

3. The blood stains on the Shroud show the effects of Crucifixion. Blood stains on the back torso and legs are consistent with wounds made by a Roman *flagrum.*

4. The wounds on the head are puncture wounds consistent with a crown or helmet of thorns.

5. The image on the Shroud is a negative one, something that artists of the first century knew nothing about because photography would not be invented for another 1800 years.

6. The image does not permeate the fabric but is only present on the very tops or crowns of the fibrils.

7. When photographed, the image produces more information than can be seen with the naked eye.

8. The Scriptures tell us that Christ's body was wrapped in a burial cloth and that there was also a cloth wrapped around Jesus' head. The Shroud of Turin and the Sudarium of Oviedo corroborate these cloths, which are mentioned in the Gospel of John 20: 5-7.

9. The Shroud of Turin and the Sudarium of Oviedo have numerous convergence points, which show they were present in the same place at the same time and touched the same body.

10. No one can explain how the image was imprinted on the cloth other than by the event of the Resurrection.

In a court of law, the overwhelming accumulation of evidence would close the case for the Resurrection of Jesus Christ. The proofs for the authenticity of the Shroud of Turin are substantial. But the implications of the Resurrection of Christ are so far-reaching and so personal, that the case remains open for each individual to decide.

For those who believe, their lives will never be the same. They will live in the knowledge of John 11: 25-26, where Jesus himself tells us, "I am the Resurrection and the life. He who believes in me will live, even though he dies; and whoever lives and believes in me will never die. Do you believe this?"

Endnotes

1   Dr. Edgar Mitchell, Interview, *The Fabric of Time*, DVD, David W. Balsiger, Senior Producer, Grizzly Adams Productions, Inc., 2006.

WHAT DO CHRISTIANS BELIEVE ABOUT SALVATION?

by Joette Whims

Is the Resurrection a fact of history? Who is Jesus? Why did he come to earth? How did he leave this earth? The apostle Paul gives us this explanation:

> I delivered to you first of all that which also I received: that Christ died for our sins according to the Scriptures, and that he was buried, and that he rose again on the third day according to the Scriptures, and that he was seen by Cephas [Peter], then by the twelve. After that he was seen by over five hundred brethren at once, of whom the greater part remain to the present, but some have fallen asleep. After that he was seen by James, then by all the apostles. Then last of all he was seen by me also, as by one born out of due time (1 Corin. 15:3-8).

Paul wanted to make sure that people understood the truth of the Resurrection and the importance of Christ living today. In fact, the Resurrection is so vital the very foundation of Christianity hangs on its truth. Paul explains:

> Now if Christ is preached that he has been raised from the dead, how do some among you say that there is no Resurrection of the dead? But if there is no Resurrection of the dead, then Christ is not risen. And if Christ is not risen, then our preaching is empty and your faith is also empty. ... And if Christ is not risen, your faith is futile; you are still in your sins!" (1 Corin. 15:12-14, 17).

The Resurrection opened the way for people to believe the following truths:

1. Jesus is God. He proved this by rising from the dead (Matthew 20:19-23).

2. Jesus has the power to forgive sins (1 John 2:2).

3. Each person must be "born again" to experience God's forgiveness (John 3:1-18).

4. A person receives a new life when he receives Christ as Savior (1 Corin. 15:21, 22).

5. Each individual is assured of eternal life when he asks Jesus to forgive his sins (Romans 6:11).

6. Each person who believes becomes a child of God (John 1:10-13).

Either the Resurrection is a fact of history, or Christ cannot be the One who took the sins of the world upon himself so that men and women can live with God forever. The Resurrection is the hope for eternal life! And it is this great hope to which the Shroud of Turin attests as a "silent witness."

Thomas was the disciple who doubted the Resurrection. He said that if he could just see the imprint of the nails on Jesus' hands and feet he would believe. Not long after that rash statement, Jesus appeared to Thomas and told him to touch the nail scars on his hands and feet. Thomas's reaction was to kneel and worship Jesus. (See John 20.) If Jesus did rise from the dead, then he truly must be God and deserves to be worshiped.

The Bible teaches that one who believes on Jesus should practice a life of discipline, which includes gathering with other believers regularly, prayer, and reading the Bible. Because Jesus was raised from the dead, he assures each person who believes in him that the believer will live forever. Therefore the future is not dark, but alive with joy and hope.

The empty tomb is the foundation of Christianity and what separates it from every other religion. And because of the empty tomb, each person on earth can have hope through believing and trusting in Jesus Christ.

A LAWYER ARGUES THE AUTHENTICITY OF THE SHROUD OF TURIN

by Michael Minor. Esq.

The Shroud of Turin is either the burial cloth of the historic Jesus of Nazareth or it is the most clever fraud and forgery ever perpetrated by the hand of man. It is one of the other; there's no middle ground. There are hundreds of pieces of scientific and historical evidence that support the authenticity of the Shroud. There's only one piece of evidence that says the Shroud is not authentic, which is the 1988 Carbon-14 test. However, Carbon-

14 testing has, itself, been much disputed. If I were going to make the case for the authenticity of the Shroud in a court of law, I would give a jury argument along the following lines:

• The Shroud of Turin is a piece of ancient linen cloth with herringbone weave. It is approximately 14 ½ feet long and 3 ½ feet wide. It is now housed in Turin's Cathedral of St. John the Baptist. The Shroud of Turin contains the faint sepia image of a naked man, bearing all the marks of Jesus' Crucifixion.

• Jesus' Crucifixion was unique among Crucifixion victims. The image of the naked corpse contains wounds that are consistent with those described in the gospel accounts of Jesus' Crucifixion. The Shroud contains puncture wounds on the scalp which, of course, would be consistent with a Crown of Thorns. There is a wound in the anatomical right side which is the exact width of a first-century Roman lance. The Shroud contains wounds on the wrists and feet consistent with nails. It contains abrasion marks on the shoulders consistent with having carried a heavy object. The Shroud also shows more than a hundred scourge marks on the torso and legs, which precisely match those made by a Roman *flagrum* or whip.

• There are imprints of coins on the eye areas. One coin was minted by Pontius Pilate only between 29 and 33 AD. It contains a rare misspelling that was unknown to numismatists until the image of this coin was discovered on the anatomical right eye of the Shroud. The anatomical left eye of the Shroud has the imprint of a Julia lepton, which was minted only in 29 AD in honor of Caesar's mother.

• The presence on the Shroud, and particularly on the bloody foot area, of a rare type limestone known as Travertine Aragonite, which is found in a small radius in and around Jerusalem, proves that the Shroud has, at some point, been in or near Jerusalem. The Shroud also contains imprints of a number of flowers which are indigenous to Palestine and bloom only during the months of March and April, the traditional period of the Passover and Crucifixion. The flower images on the Shroud appear as they would look after having been plucked for 24 to 36 hours, but not as long as 72 hours, which is consistent with the amount of time the body would have been in the tomb. Pollen grains from the flowers whose images appear on the Shroud have also been found on the Shroud as well as pollen from Gundelia Tunaforte, the Crown of Thrown plant. Interestingly, none of the pollens are coated with tempera, which is strong evidence that the Shroud image is not painted on the fabric.

• The image on the Shroud reflects rigor mortis, but not putrefaction, which indicates that the body was in the grave from 24 to 36 hours, but not as long as 72 hours. The blood areas on the Shroud are real human blood, contain hemoglobin and give a positive test for serum albumen. There is no image under the blood stains, which indicates the blood was on the Shroud *before* the image was imprinted, which is as it should be. The image is a negative image, which becomes a positive image when photographed, and is only on the very crowns of the fibrils with a three-percent contrast, almost the limit of visibility. Also, the image on the Shroud has no directionality, capillarity, brush strokes or pigment, all of which factors would be present if the Shroud were a painting. Additionally, there are no shadows or outlines on the Shroud, which all works of art and paintings necessarily have.

• The positions of the Crucifixion victim on the cross can be calculated from the blood flow on the arms and other parts of the body, which follow the laws of gravity and blood circulation. These physiological laws were not discovered until 1693 and 1666 AD respectively. Very significantly, ethnologists and anthropologists have identified the man of the Shroud as being of Semitic origin and in his early thirties. One of the indices of this ethnic group are the peyuses, or sidelocks of hair, which are visible on either side of the face of the man of the Shroud and which are unique to Jewish men.

• The Gospel accounts relate that Joseph of Arimathea, a disciple of Jesus, purchased a fine, clean linen cloth with which to wrap the body of Jesus. Joseph also provided a new or unused tomb in which to lay the body. It was highly unusual for a Crucifixion victim to be placed in a tomb at all, much less wrapped in fine linen. The bodies of crucifixion victims were normally unceremoniously thrown into a mass grave.

• Images of fingers, but not of the thumbs, are visible on the Shroud. An artist or forger would have had to have known that putting nails through the wrists damage the median nerves, which in turn, causes the thumbs to involuntarily reflex inward toward the palms. Placing nails in the wrists instead of the palms is contrary to both Christian art and tradition. However, nails through the palms would not have supported the weight of the body, and would have torn free.

• The reputed D'Arcis Memorandum has never been proven to be genuine. None of the copies of the D'Arcis Memorandum that we have are either signed or dated, and there's no proof that the Pope ever saw the Memorandum, or that it was ever delivered to him. Additionally, no trace or hint of the identity of the purported artist has ever been found. Whoever the purported artist was, his talent would have been far greater than that of Michelangelo, Rafael, and da Vinci combined. The D'Arcis Memorandum lacks any probative value for several reasons. Most convincing to me is the fact that it is neither signed nor dated. Moreover, there is no evidence that it is even in the handwriting of the bishop that it is purported to be, and it is simply estimated to be "circa" or about 1389 AD. The artist or forger isn't identified, and there is no transcript or any sort of investigation, official or otherwise.

• Photographs of the Shroud are unique in science and in art, having three-dimensional distance information encoded in them when subjected into them when subjected to a VP-8 Analyzer, which is a device used to study photographs from outer space. No other known photographs have such distance information encoded into them or three-dimensional qualities.

• After thousands of hours of scientific testing, the STURP team, which included some of the premiere scientists in the world, concluded that the image on the Shroud is that of a real human man who was scourged and crucified. It is not the product of an artist. Also, the peer-reviewed work of Ray Rogers, a respected chemist formerly with Los Alamos National Laboratory, strongly suggests that the Carbon-14 date of the Shroud is inaccurate because the tested Shroud sample was taken from a patched *and* rewoven area of the Shroud. Space-age science and technology still do not know how the image on the Shroud of Turin was formed, or how to duplicate the image. While there is no fingerprint for Jesus, it is not logical, empirical, or scientific to ignore literally hundreds of pieces of scientific and historical evidence and conclude that the Shroud is not genuine based on only a single piece of evidence, radioCarbon-14, which is itself now much in dispute. More importantly, according to Ray Rogers' work, it was a patched and rewoven area that was carbon-dated and not the actual Shroud.

The circumstantial evidence in support of the authenticity of the Shroud of Turin is simply overwhelming. In my professional opinion, it would meet the most stringent evidentiary requirements in a court of law *beyond a reasonable doubt.*

If the Shroud now housed in Turin's Cathedral of St. John the Baptist is not the burial cloth of the historic Jesus of Nazareth, then who is it and what is it? It is either the most clever medieval forgery ever perpetrated by the hand of man or it is the burial cloth of the historic Jesus of Nazareth. It is one or the other; there is no middle ground. You be the jury.

THE SHROUD AND IMAGE ATTRIBUTES

*by Thomas D'Muhala and
Alan Whanger, M.D.*

1. The Shroud bears an image of a crucified man, consistent with the Gospel accounts.

2. The image is so faint, it is impossible to differentiate between some anatomical features at distances less than several feet. If it were a painting, the artist would have had to use a several foot-long brush.

3. The Shroud image is a negative image; a photographic negative of the Shroud bears a positive image. However, this unique contrast reversal does not mean it is the result of some photographic process.

4. The Shroud's fully documented history began in Lirey, France in 1353, more than 500 years before the concept of negativity was known. So, if it were a painting, the artist would have had to use a several foot-long brush to paint a negative image centuries before the concept of negativity was known.

5. The image is anatomically perfect. There is no existing work of art—product

of human eye-hand coordination—that is anatomically perfect.

6. The image on the Shroud is that of a human body in rigor mortis.

7. Distance information is encoded in the image. It is a true three-dimensional image. There is no other image, in art or photography, with distance information encoded in it. It is a unique image. So, if it were a painting, the artist would have had to stand many feet back from the linen surface to paint an anatomically perfect image, in the negative, with three-dimensional information encoded in the image, several centuries before the concepts of negativity and 3-D encoding were known.

8. There is a factor of directionality to the blood flow on the wrists (nail wounds) and forearms that is consistent with the flow of blood, due to gravity, resulting from the two different positions of the Crucifixion victim on the cross. In light of Christian tradition and art, it is unlikely an artist would have thought of this fact.

9. Marks of a severe scourging of the body are evident on the Shroud. Marks on the image (wounds evidencing blood) appear to be the result of scourging with a whip, the design of

which is consistent with early-art depictions of a Roman flagrum, including dumbbell shaped weights (tortilla) on the ends of each thong. These "marks" precisely match tortilla found in archaeological excavations.

10. The scourging was savage because there are at least 120 tortilla marks covering both the frontal and dorsal images from the neck to the ankles.

11. There are multiple puncture wounds in the scalp, consistent with a crowning of thorns. There is also evidence on the image of two thorns remaining in the back of the head.

12. The blood on the Shroud is human blood.

13. The chemistry of blood-flows from scourging, crowning with thorns, and nailing to the cross show it to be blood of severe trauma, with very high bilirubin content.

14. The chemistry of the blood-flow from the wound in the side (lance wound) shows it to be post mortem blood.

15. Chemical analysis shows that blood flow from the wound in the side is separated into serum and plasma—"first blood, then water."

16. Empirical test results show that the time between each wound's bleeding and the deposit of that blood on the Shroud is consistent with the Gospel accounts.

17. The blood was deposited on the Shroud before the image was formed. There is no image information under the blood on the Shroud.

18. There appears to be a three dimensional object on each eyelid. These objects are the size of, and bear the identifiable inscriptions and images found on, Pontius Pilate lepton coins, a small coin, known as the "widow's mite" in Scripture. These coins were hand-struck in Israel between 29 and 31 AD.

19. There are pollen grains found on the Shroud, which are consistent with what is believed to be the historical geographical route of the Shroud, beginning in Jerusalem, going to Edessa, and then on eventually to Turin, Italy.

20. There are identifiable images of about 30 different flowers, thorns, thistles, leaves, and berries found on the Shroud. These findings are substantially supported by the independent identification of pollen grains found on the Shroud.

21. Many of the flower images appear to be as they would have looked 30 to 36 hours after they were picked. The only place in the world where this collection of flowers could be found in a fresh state is in the immediate vicinity of Jerusalem. Their common blooming time is March and April.

22. Some of these flower images, with their positions on the Shroud being rather accurate, are depicted on icons, such as the Christ Pantocrator of St. Catherine's Monastery in the sixth century, and on Byzantine coins such as the gold solidus of 692 AD.

23. One flower, the Capparis aegyptia, is called a "clock flower," since the bud begins opening in the morning and is fully open just before sundown. A botanist can tell the time of day by the degree of opening of the flower and its anthers. When the flower is picked, the opening immediately stops and remains at that state. The clearly identifiable images of the "clock flower" on the Shroud indicate that those flowers were picked between 3 and 4 o'clock in the afternoon of the day that they were placed within the Shroud, entirely in agreement with the scriptural accounts of

the timing of the Crucifixion, entombment, and Resurrection.

24. Two of the plants imaged on the Shroud, the thistle of Gundelia Tournefortii and the Zygophyllum dumosum, which grows only in the Sinai desert, would localize the origin of the Shroud to the immediate vicinity of Jerusalem since that is the only area where the growth boundaries overlap.

25. The legs are arched, with one foot slightly higher than the other. This is consistent with feet and leg positions associated with a Crucifixion of this type as if one foot were placed on the other to facilitate nailing to the cross.

26. There is evidence of a wound on one knee, consistent with a fall while carrying the cross.

27. The nose cartilage is dislocated, and there is a pronounced swelling of one of the cheeks (immediately below the eye), possibly the result of being struck on the face, or a fall.

28. The image resembles an auto-radiograph; it contains identifiable images of bones, teeth, eye orbits, and sinus cavities.

29. There are no dyes, pigments, or stains on the Shroud that correlate with the image.

30. Image information resides only on the top of fibrils that make up Shroud threads; and the contrast of the image information decreases as you descend down/around the sides of the fibrils, terminating at the exact side (90 degrees off top center) as if it were emblazoned on the cloth from an infinite number of point sources residing within/on the body it covered.

31. Visible image information resides only within the first few microns of the surface of each fibril.

32. The image is only on the Shroud's surface that faced toward the body There is no image information on the reverse of the cloth.

33. The blood has soaked through to the backside of the Shroud.

34. The image *appears* to be the result of some form of coherent radiant energy which emanated from the body.

35. There is remarkable correlation between the Shroud's facial image and the face of Jesus depicted on icons and coins from the sixth century on. The presence of hundreds of points of congruence between the two images would indicate that a number of the artists had

to have looked directly at the Shroud face as the model for their icons.

36. There are very early representations of Christ in the Catacombs of Domitilla and others in Rome from the end of the first, second, third and fourth centuries that are totally shroud-like.

37. The nail wounds are in the wrists, not in the hands, which is a departure from Christian tradition and art. Only in the wrists would a driven nail support the weight of a human body without breaking any bones, especially during convulsions associated with a Crucifixion of this type.

38. There is no factor of directionality in the image, no brush strokes, preferential direction or directions, etc. The image is a totally random deposit of information, which is powerful evidence contrary to it being the result of human intervention. It is not the product of human eye-hand coordination.

39. The image pixel boundaries of the Shroud image terminate abruptly, which is unique among photographs and paintings. This would seem to indicate that the image-producing mechanism was some kind of discrete, vertically directed radiation-like agent of pinpoint accuracy.

40. While the Shroud was carbon dated to the years 1260 to 1390 AD in 1988, the result is totally wrong for the Shroud. Only one sample was taken from a corner of the Shroud, and three pieces of this one sample were dated by three laboratories. Subsequent Pyrolysis-mass-spectrometry coupled with microscopic and microchemical studies show clearly that the area from which the sample was taken was carefully rewoven, most likely in the 16th century when rather extensive repairs were undertaken on the Shroud after damage from a fire in 1532. Other data from several sources would indicate that the Shroud actually dates from the spring of 30 AD, in the immediate vicinity of Jerusalem.

New Scientific Findings on the 3-D Image

Three-dimensional holographic front and back images of the Shroud, produced for the first time by Dr. Petrus Soons, reveal new findings and details never before seen on the Shroud of Turin or on previous two-dimensional Shroud photographs. The holograms also confirm earlier Shroud findings and speculations.

New findings include the following:

1) The position of the feet and the legs were never clearly visible in photographs. The holograms reveal that both legs were arched and one foot was bent diagonally and the toes pointing toward the side (as they would appear if fixed against the vertical beam of a cross).

The hologram reveals that one foot was positioned over the other foot, bending the leg at the knee. This was not clearly visible in any photographs taken prior to the holograms. On the holograms, the toes of both feet are visible; these were not fully visible in the photographs.

2) On previous Shroud photographs, a bloodspot appears to be floating above the area of the head. The holograms clarify that this bloodspot is actually *on top* of the head, and probably due to a wound caused by a *helmet* of thorns. This indicates that the crown of thorns was more cap-like than circular.

3) In the holographic images, the marks caused by the dumbbell-shaped weights on the end of a Roman *flagrum* (whip) follow the curves on the sides of the upper and lower legs as well as the shoulders—these curvatures could never have been faked in a painting.

4) The holographic images exhibit two small solid objects on the eyelids. These objects are believed by some Shroud researchers to be small coins, minted between 29 to 33 AD.

5) The holographic images clearly show the details of the sides of the face which were not visible in conventional photographs.

6) The holograms validate other major findings, including the swelling under the right eye and the localization of the bloodspots throughout the body.

7) On the back of the head in previous two-dimensional photographs, researchers observed what appeared to be a ponytail. The holographic images appear to confirm this speculation … although Dr. Soons believes the hologram shows a hairline in the back, so that what seemed to be a ponytail appears to be an artifact in the Shroud textile itself.

8) In the past, the beard was believed to be bifurcated (divided at the bottom). It is thought by some Shroud researchers that the holograms indicate this is not the case, as an intact beard is visible in the holographic image.

The discoloring and darkening of the moustache and beard may be due to fluid that came out of the mouth and nose from the lungs (lung edema) when the body was taken down from the cross and laid in a horizontal position. Also visible is the direction of the fluid flow, from right above to left below. A portion of the right side of the moustache and the central portion of the beard did not receive this edema lung fluid and consequently does not show this discoloring and darkening.

9) Under the beard, on the neck area of the frontal Shroud image, the holographic images reveal the presence of a solid flat object, measuring about 4.5 by 2.5 inches. In the opinion of Dr. Soons, the object appears to have three two-inch-high Hebrew or Aramaic letters on its surface.

WHY THE SHROUD OF TURIN IS NOT A PAINTING

by Dame Isabel Piczek

Serious researchers and skeptics alike have long sought to explain just how the image of a crucified man got on the Shroud of Turin. "On the Shroud" is the appropriate term since nowhere does the image penetrate the fabric. Instead, it seems to rest on the top-most fibrils that make up the fibers of the fabric. This is an important part of the mystery since no known technology exists that is capable of replicating that effect. But one of the most persistent claims of the skeptics is that the image on the Shroud is merely a painting.

In one particularly puzzling attempt to further the notion that the image is a painting, a television documentary produced in 2005 suggested that, not only is it a painting, but it was actually painted by Leonardo da Vinci. Yet Da Vinci would not be born for one hundred years after the Shroud's first known public exhibition in Lire, France.

Dame Piczek is a monumental artist with hundreds of paintings adorning churches, cathedrals, and other buildings all over the world. She is also a particle physicist and thinks that this idea is absolutely absurd. She commented on the issue:

There are many lesser arguments about the veracity of the Shroud of Turin, but referring specifically to the notion that Leonardo da Vinci painted the Shroud, it should be obvious that he could not have done so. He was born a hundred years after the first exhibition of the Shroud, and his personal painting techniques are well-known.

He was an extremely slow painter, unable to master the techniques of fresco painting. That was the tragedy of *The Last Supper,* which started to peel during his lifetime. The mural of *The Battle of Anghian* started to run and was destroyed while he was still working on it. Unfortunately, most of the great Master's works are in a varying state of preservation because of his slow and very layered technique, which he employed without exception. The Shroud has absolutely no paint layers. There is absolutely no chance that Leonardo da Vinci would have, or could have, painted it, even if it was a painting.

In all of the detailed notebooks kept by Leonardo, who recorded even such minute details as a shoe lace he bought for one of his students, there is not one drawing, not even a sentence that would hint at any work on a shroud-like project. Yet, in an attempt to give the theory a veneer of modern science, the producers of this documentary suggested that the art of photography must have actually been invented 600 years before it was a recognized technology for the very purpose of creating the image on the Shroud. The implication was that their experiments proved the thesis. In fact, according to some who were involved in the production of the television documentary, the experiments were all total failures, which proved, of course, the exact opposite.

The Leonardo da Vinci theory presents yet another dilemma for those who cling to it. Either the entire history of the Mandylion, which predates da Vinci by hundreds of years, must be discarded or otherwise explained or one must suppose that there were two Shrouds—the one touched by King Abgar and brought by force of arms to Constantinople and the other painted by da Vinci.

There have been a number of other attempts to portray the image as a painting, all of them unsuccessful. Dr. Walter McCrone perhaps did more to further this idea than anyone before or since. He claimed as an absolute fact that the Shroud was a painting. He said that he found on the Shroud through the use of microscopy pigments and a paint medium that artists used in the Middle Ages.

Dr. McCrone has credentials as a scientist, particularly as a polarized light microscopist. He graduated from Cornell University with a PhD in chemical microscopy, and, as the director of McCrone Associates, devoted his life to this direct method of scientific investigation. He uncovered a number of high profile artistic forgeries. He wrote a book about his Shroud research called *Judgment Day for the Shroud.* However, there are many others equally well-known and respected who disagree with McCrone's views.

Dr. McCrone, prior to his death, was absolutely convinced that he was right and the rest of the scientists who disagreed with him were wrong. He even predicted that some future scientist, around the year 2279, would completely vindicate his findings. Indeed, he felt that the 1988 carbon dating results had already vindicated his unyielding assertion that the Shroud image was hand-painted by an artist in 1355. He based this date upon the D'Arcis Memorandum. Why is it, then, that Father Renaldi, with whom McCrone conducted a lengthy and ongoing correspondence relative to the Shroud, once warned him that he was viewed as "the adversary?" Could it be because Dr. McCrone assumed an adversarial position?

With regard to the blood stains on the Shroud, for example, McCrone dismissed the work of Drs. Heller and Adler, both highly regarded scientists, by saying simply, "There is *no* [his emphasis] blood on the Shroud." And added, "Obviously, I amuse myself by thinking of Heller and Adler as STURP Shroudies, who found blood everywhere on the Shroud." (Neither Heller nor Adler were members of the STRUP team in 1978 when the Shroud was examined.)

For his conclusions, Dr. McCrone relied almost exclusively on observations with a polarized light microscope, although he welcomed corroborations from microscopists using the more modern electron microscope. Former student Ray Rogers concluded, "The image does not reside in an applied pigment. The reflectance, fluorescence, and chemical characteristics of the Shroud image indicate that the image-recording mechanism involved some cellulose oxidation dehydration process."

Dr. McCrone responded by saying, "I should ask Ray to return his certificate for successful completion of my course in polarized microscopy, which he took in 1959."

How then did Dr. McCrone explain the negative aspect of the image and the fact of the three-dimensional quality? In yet another reply to a letter from Father Peter Renaldi, who very pointedly asked the same question, Dr. McCrone wrote, "I feel the negative character of the image is a coincidence resulting from the artist's conception of his commission. I feel it is also a coincidence that the negative image yields a three-dimensional figure. This is a natural consequence of the artist's effort to produce a body image based on contact points."

So according to Dr. McCrone, the Shroud image is a painting, period, and the scientific anomalies so far discovered are merely coincidences. Unfortunately, that notion, no matter how elegantly phrased, simply does not hold up. Father Renaldi repeatedly asked Dr. McCrone to discuss his findings with a qualified art expert, but McCrone wasn't interested. "My problem with a serious dialogue with qualified art experts," he wrote," is finding one that I regard as an expert. The Shroud is not a question for art experts."

But as an art expert, I can assure everyone that the Turin Shroud is not a painting or an artifact made by man. Dr. McCrone's analysis refers to *synovia* or *synochre,* particles of Venetian red, a common medieval paint component that he says he found on the fabric. The claim was also made by Dr. McCrone that the Shroud was painted with greatly diluted glue tempera. Glue erratically reacts to atmospheric changes; therefore, it is used only with chemical stabilizers. If none can be found on the Shroud sticky tapes, then it is not a glue paint medium. In its most diluted form, the medium does not permanently hold the paint particles. Also, this medium remains absolutely water soluble. In the case of a highly diluted medium, one does not have to dislodge paint particles. They are loosely attached because of the unpleasant qualities of this medium. That is why this technique was seldom used for fine art.

Dr. McCrone takes his knowledge of medieval paint techniques from old books and art authors such as Senino, Senini, and Eastlake. The words *synopisi* or *synochre* used by McCrone are not in use today, and Venetian red is an arbitrary term used for the unknown *synochre*. The professional arts strongly state that the Shroud is not a painting or man-made artifact. The Shroud is much, much more than any one of us could even start to understand.

One might think that would put the theory to rest, but not so. Dr. McCrone's influence reaches out from beyond the grave. In September of 2006, a major network took their cameras into the McCrone Group, and the subjects of the Shroud of Turin along with the Vinland Map were both raised as major hoaxes uncovered by McCrone's particular brand of microscopy. Dr. McCrone's legend and his propensity to perpetuate that legend as indisputable fact live on. The representative to whom the reporter spoke began by saying that they had examined 88,000 particles and fibers from the Shroud and had determined unequivocally that the image was a painting. The interviewer seemed satisfied with that, and apparently never thought to ask if 88,000 particles and fibers wouldn't have used up the entire fabric. According to Tom D'Muhala, president of STURP at the time, who pointed out that that number was off by a factor of nearly 50. Dr. Frei, in collecting his samples, was hoping to find dust and pollens that might have been ingrained deeply in the fibers. He pressed firmly with his thumb and forefinger, and as a result, picked up an average of 100 fibrils and particles on each of his tapes.

STURP, on the other hand, was looking for anomalies in the fibrils themselves, so they put much less pressure when applying the tape. They averaged only 50 particles and fibrils per tape. According to Dr. Alan Whanger, who is the custodian of Dr. Frei's samples, there are a total of 27 tape samples in the Frei collection, which as far as can be determined, McCrone never had access to. And there are a total of 38 tape samples in the STURP collection, 37 of which are from the Shroud and 1 from the Holland backing cloth. These were the samples loaned to Dr. McCrone by Ray Rogers. All of these sticky tape samples still exist. So, even if the Frei collection is included, and assuming Dr. McCrone examined every particle and fibril in the STURP collection, that amounts to only a grand total of 1,850 possible particles and fibrils available to McCrone. That is a long way from 88,000.

The truth is that Dr. McCrone's polarized light microscope saw far less of the Shroud than his company now represents. And at no time did Dr. McCrone or anyone else ever make a microscopic examination of the entire image.

Television program moderators are asking physicists, chemists, medical experts, the corner druggist, and high school teachers this question—Is the Shroud a painting?—and of course, the answer is always wrong. First, a painting always is the result of an educated, conscious, and intelligent activity. It is never a strange, single item. It faultlessly fits into the cultural era of the times in which it was made. The Turin Shroud does not fit this definition at all. In spite of what lay people hope to be true, a painting does not depend on paint particles. It thoroughly and solely depends on the paint mediums, binders in liquid forms, mediums that tie the paint particles to each other and to the paint background. This creates a continuous film that alone carries the image consciously willed by the painter to appear on the surface. By natural law, it can only be a visible and continuous image while the medium remains intact. Once it starts to disintegrate, chunks of the image or the painting will be missing.

The image on the Shroud of Turin is an intact, continuous image without any continuous paint medium fill. This is the strongest and most definite proof that the Shroud is not a painting. This very fact alone is enough to kill the painting accusation. If an image on a painting could exist without a continuous medium paint film, it would be a greater miracle than the Shroud itself. It would go against all the laws of nature.

If the Mandylion and the Shroud of Turin are one and the same cloth, it has survived flood, fire, several wars, and 2,000 years of being folded, unfolded, damaged, and repaired. Could a painting with a highly diluted water-based glue tempera survive such an ordeal? Especially one painted on a piece of fabric? Could it last 700 years or even 100 years?

In the end, it appears that Dr. McCrone convinced no one but himself and the heirs to his company he founded that the image was or is a painting. In spite of the fact that he loudly and persistently held his observations and analyses to be superior to some of the world's leading hematologists, nuclear scientists, particle physicists, chemists, biologists, space scientists, computer experts, photographic and fabric specialists, and dozens of other scientific experts, including other microscopists, not one of them agreed with him.

The official summary of STURP findings is explicit, "After several years of exhaustive study and evaluation of the data, STURP officially concludes no pigments, paints, dyes, or stains have been found on the fibrils. X-ray fluorescence and microchemistry on the fibrils preclude the possibility of paint being used as a method for creating the image. Ultraviolet and infrared evaluations confirm these studies. A scientific consensus is: There are no chemical or physical methods known which can account for the totality of the image, nor can any combination of physical, chemical, biological, or medical circumstances explain the image adequately."

The hard, inescapable fact is that the STURP conclusion still stands. And in spite of a number of challenges, no attempt to reproduce the image on the Shroud of Turin has yet been successful, or even come close. But there is one certainty in all of this, and that is that the image exists. It is visible, resting on matter that can be touched, examined, tested, and analyzed, which it has been far more than any other artifact. That fact, that certainty, requires an answer from those who insist that it simply could not be the burial Shroud of the crucified Jesus of Nazareth.

If the Shroud of Turin is not a painting, and if modern scientists and artists cannot reproduce it, then what is it and why is it there?

FLOWER IMAGES ON THE SHROUD

by Dr. Alan and Mary Whanger

The marvelous images of the crucified and resurrected Jesus on the Shroud of Turin are obviously the central and crucial features, but there are also on the Shroud the frail and often fragmentary images of many objects associated with the Passion, the Crucifixion, and the enshroudment and entombment. We are fortunate in having about 30 very high-grade enhanced photographs of the Shroud made from the photographs taken by Giuseppe Enrie in 1931. These images are often so faint on later photographs that they are very difficult for most people to see. The images are mostly in the negative and are characteristic of corona or electrostatic discharge, thus making them much harder to perceive. There are about 30 different varieties of identified plants imaged on the Shroud. We will discuss only the floral images here because of their special relevance for the Shroud.

Faint but accurately placed images of flowers and 7th century Byzantine coins can be seen on 6th century icons of Jesus. In addition, they are depicted on medieval art work. However, the first written comments on the flower images, as far as I (Alan) have been able to determine, were from Oswald Scheuermann, with whom I worked on a corona image formation theory. In 1983 he wrote that he thought he saw some flower images around the face. I looked at some of our photographs, and I did not perceive them. I wrote him that I was not sure what he was referring to, and since we were already embroiled in controversies about the coin images over the eyes, suggested that we "back burner" the flower issue.

In 1985, I was closely examining a small detail on one of our Enrie photographs when I became aware of what seemed like a circle of small faces. On backing off, I saw immediately that they were petals of a flower about 2 ½ inches in diameter lateral to and just above the anatomic left side of the forehead. I called my wife, Mary, to look, and she immediately saw the pattern when it was pointed out. Once realizing what flower images look like on the Shroud, we examined the photographs again, and noted many other similar images of various flowers. I contacted Scheuermann again with this news, and over the next months, he skillfully made corona images off a variety of flowers and plants and other objects. These were of enormous help in being able to perceive these complex images on the Shroud.

Since we do not have a background in botany, identifying these images was a great problem. Fortunately, another of our colleagues, Rex Morgan, was in Jerusalem at that time, and he procured the multiple volumes of the *Flora Palaestina,* the definitive botany books of Israel. Then began the tedious task of trying to match the images on the Shroud with the life-size drawings in the books. It took us about four years to tentatively identify 28 different varieties of flowers and plants imaged on the Shroud. Of these, twenty-three are flowers, three are bushes, and two are thorns. We felt that these were important for Shroud research, since all of these grow in the Near East in the vicinity of Jerusalem; the common blooming time was March and April; and our studies and those of Scheuermann indicated that many of these had the appearance that would be expected about thirty to thirty-six hours after having been picked.

In addition, the previous and independent work by Dr. Max Frei, who had taken sticky tape samples off the Shroud in 1973 and 1978 for pollen grain examination, had identified 58 varieties of pollen grains. Of these, most were from plants growing in the regions of Jerusalem, a number were from other parts of the Middle East, especially the region of Edessa, and a number were of European origin. Of the twenty-eight floral images on the Shroud, Frei had identified the pollen grains of twenty-five of these at least to the genus level and mostly to the species.

We tried to get these results into the media and into print, but this was 1989, and the radiocarbon dating test done on the Shroud in 1988 had reported that the Shroud originated between 1260 and 1390 and hence was a fake. That news was spread worldwide by the media, who have been rather hostile to the Shroud anyway, and this made it impossible to get any of our findings published or shown.

Our other research had already shown that the Shroud originated in the region of Jerusalem in the spring of the year AD 30, so we knew that the carbon dating was grossly in error. The big question was how the date could be so far wrong. We obtained a video of the taking of the single sample in 1988, and observed on a frame-by-frame analysis of the video that there were stiff and abnormal threads running through the piece taken for the sample. It was apparent to us then, and has been subsequently proved by multiple examinations, that indeed the piece taken for the testing had been extensively rewoven, probably in the 16th century. Thus the radiocarbon test for the Shroud is totally invalid, although many still resist acknowledging this.

We basically had to sit on this fascinating information about the botanical findings until 1995 when we joined a Shroud group touring

Israel. I had heard about Dr. Avinoam Danin, Professor of Botany at Hebrew University in Jerusalem, and world authority on the flora of the Near East. I telephoned him before starting our trip, indicating that I was a researcher on the Shroud and I had found some floral images that I would like for him to look at, to which he agreed. We took several of our photographs to Israel with us and went to his home in Jerusalem. After getting acquainted, I handed him the photographs on which I had first noted the flowers, but did not indicate what I had found during our four years of searching. Professor Danin looked at the photographs for about 15 seconds and said: "Those are the flowers of Jerusalem."

That is what I thought, but it was reassuring to have the world authority on the flowers of Jerusalem agree with us. He knew immediately that this was no ordinary finding, and he agreed to work with us.

Professor Danin has visited us in North Carolina on six occasions, spending over a month with us, going over our photographs and the various specimens and materials in Dr. Frei's collection. In 1988 we had acquired Dr. Frei's entire collection from Mrs. Frei except for some specimens that apparently had gotten lost in Italy somewhere, and brought it back to the United States so that we could continue some studies on it. In addition, he arranged for Dr. Uri Baruch, a palynologist (pollen expert) with the Israeli Antiquities Authority, to come here twice to reexamine the Frei slides for the pollen grains. Exacting identification of the pollen grains, which are still stuck in the adhesive tape, is technically difficult, but Dr. Baruch was able to identify 204 pollen grains of 33 different types of pollens on scanning the tapes. This material was incorporated into a monograph entitled *Flora of the Shroud of Turin,* jointly authored by A. Danin, A. Whanger, U. Baruch, and M. Whanger, and published by the Missouri Botanical Press.

Professor Danin has given scientific presentations on the flora of the Shroud at a number of Shroud conferences and other meetings. Interestingly, in 2006, large permanent Shroud exhibitions opened in Jerusalem and in Rome, and Professor Danin gave the inaugural addresses at both exhibitions and contributed materials of our floral findings for two exhibition panels.

Professor Danin concurred with most of our floral identifications and has made several new ones, which include three thistles and two thorns. Small fruits of the *Pistacia lentiscus* are visible and were part of the burial spices. In addition, one of the plants that Professor Danin identified, the *Capparis aegyptia*, flowers in a very particular way. The bud begins opening mid-morning and opens progressively during the day until it is fully open just before sundown. A botanist can tell the time of the day by the degree of opening of the bud. The opening ceases immediately when the flower is picked.

Danin stated that this flower as shown on the Shroud was picked between three and four o'clock in the afternoon, corresponding precisely with the time that preparations for the entombment of the body had gotten underway according to the Biblical accounts. He concurred that the common blooming time is March and April, and that the only place in the entire world where this particular grouping of flowers could be found in a fresh state is in the immediate vicinity of Jerusalem. There are masses of flowers on the Shroud, but most are too wilted and clumped together to be identifiable. There are several bouquets of flowers on and around the body.[1]

Thus the botanical findings give us a great amount of information to help us better understand and appreciate the Shroud and its marvelous message. They help us to locate the origin of the Shroud in Jerusalem during March or April, the time of the Passover. The findings also demonstrate the torture and humiliation of the Crown of Thorns forced onto the head of Jesus. However, they indicate the loving care of family and friends in gathering flowers and bouquets in the late afternoon to offset the ugliness of the Crucifixion. They show that spices were gathered to offset the anticipated stench of decay; and they disclose that it was about 30 to 36 hours after the flowers were picked that some extraordinary event occurred that left the still unexplained complex radiation images of the body and the flowers on the Shroud for our information and inspiration.

Endnotes

1 Professor Danin has an excellent website illustrating many of the floral and pollen images and related finding: http://www.botanic.co.il/A/articls/WebFlshrd_files/frame.htm

Council for Study of the Shroud of Turin
P.O. Box 3190, Durham, NC 27715-3190
www.shroudcouncil.org
Chairman, Alan D. Whanger, MD

THE SUDARIUM—
FACE CLOTH OF JESUS

by Mark Guscin

One of the of the most significant developments in Shroud studies over the last few years has been the emergence of another linen cloth, a smaller one known as the Sudarium of Oviedo. Oviedo is a small cathedral town in the north of Spain, and this is the site of where the Sudarium has been preserved for centuries. This cloth does not contain any images but has many blood stains. Many believe that this is the cloth that was wrapped around the head of the Lord during his Crucifixion.

A Sudarium was generally made of linen, but very poor quality material like this one, which has threads hanging out of it. They were not very well made because their use was not the same as a good quality linen cloth sold as a burial cloth. "Sudarium" is a difficult word to translate into English because none of the translations convey everything to our mind that the word would have conveyed to a first century Roman. The word comes from the Latin for "sweat." Sweat cloth is perhaps one of the uses of these cloths. People either carried them around their necks or tied to their wrists to use them to clean the dust off their faces. We know from the Roman poet Marchel that the cloths were also used in barber shops. As far as we know, cloths like this with claims to have been used during the Resurrection have survived, but this one has always been special because it's always been referred to in historical documents as the Sudarium of the Lord.

We know about the Sudarium from classical sources such as Suitonius and the poet Catullus, who used the word Sudarium. Suitonius tells us that the Emperor Nero wrapped a Sudarium around his mouth to protect himself from infections and germs and to protect his voice when he wanted to be a professional singer.

Description of the Cloth

Tests on the Sudarium have revealed that this cloth was used to wrap the head of the corpse of an adult male with long hair and a long beard. This person had been severely tortured before dying, which is made evident by the different types of blood on the cloth, including blood shed while the person was living and postmortem blood. The man whose head was wrapped in the cloth died in an upright position with his arms outstretched, which is perfectly compatible with Crucifixion. This person also died of asphyxiation, which is the primary cause of death in Crucifixion.

Tests on the cloth also show that the corpse laid in a horizontal position face-down on the ground for approximately one hour. After that, the body was picked up and moved for about 5 to 10 minutes. Then, for some reason, the cloth was taken off the head. All of this information has come out through the painstaking, very, very careful reproduction of all of the stains on the cloth.

It's fascinating to examine an item that on first sight looks like a dirty, stained piece of cloth. In fact, the testing team's forensic doctor commented, "If you saw something like that in the street, you would just avoid even touching it if you could." I was amazed when I thought about how that cloth was used and how the different blood stains were formed on it. While there is an image on the Shroud, there is no image on the Sudarium. That's because the Sudarium was taken off the head before the body was placed in the Shroud and before the Resurrection, which created the image on the Shroud. That's exactly what John describes in chapter 20 of his Gospel. In a rather ambiguous phrase in Greek that literally means "in one place" or "in a place," he says the face cloth was separate, not with the other linen cloth. In the same verse, the Gospel repeats that the face cloth was not with the larger burial cloth.

History of the Sudarium

From my point of view as a historian, it was fascinating to track down all the different manuscripts in the archives, collecting the known history, correcting previous readings, and putting the history into order. Would anyone spend so much time and effort on such an object if it wasn't related to the historical person of Jesus of Nazareth?

The history of the Sudarium is well documented. Manuscripts from various countries from various centuries collaborate the basic details. The historical information about who kept the Shroud of Turin in its early history is a bit garbled and confusing, and some of the sources don't agree with each other. In the case of the Sudarium, the sources are unanimous. Various independent

Eastern sources written in Syria say that Peter took the Sudarium from the tomb. It was in Jerusalem until the seventh century. This is confirmed by references from the third and fourth centuries and from a group of Italian pilgrims in the year 570. When the Persians invaded that area in the beginning of the seventh century, they took relics to use as leverage for negotiations For example, they captured a piece of what was considered to be the true cross and used it for negotiations. Eventually, the Christians recovered the cloth and various other possessions and took them across the Mediterranean to Spain.

First, the cloth was located in Seville, then Palada. In the eighth century when the Arabs invaded Spain and conquered most of the country, the Sudarium was taken to northern Spain; it's been there ever since. The city of Oviedo wasn't founded until the eighth century, but the cloth has been there ever since. For centuries, no one paid much attention to the Sudarium. When Pope John Paul II visited Oviedo in the 1980's, he wasn't told about this cloth.

The Pilgrim's Road

When the Spanish Center for Sindonology (Shroud studies) was founded in the late 1980's, the group was informed about the possible face cloth of Christ in Spain. In the 1960s, it had been examined by an Italian cleric, Monsignor Ricci. He suggested that this could well be the face cloth that is mentioned in the fourth Gospel (John) as one of the cloths that the women and the disciples saw on Easter morning. In the early 1990s, an investigation team of about forty people, mostly Spanish, examined the cloth. Everyone worked within their own scientific field, so there was no overlapping of tests or people reaching opinions about something they didn't know anything about. There were textile experts, conservation experts, chemists, forensic doctors, and a historian (myself). We've had hands-on access to the cloth the last 16 or 17 years.

As part of my special responsibility as historian of the team, I went all over Europe to find manuscripts that mention the Sudarium and to publish editions of these manuscripts in Latin with translations into Spanish and English. I found them in archives and various different places in Spain, and strangely enough, there is a relatively high concentration of manuscripts that talk about the Sudarium in the northeast of France and in Belgium. This is first time that these manuscripts have all been published together.

Many of these references go back to the medieval Pilgrim's Road, a trail that led from the Mediterranean to Santiago de Compostella. During the Middle Ages, Christians would visit three main pilgrimage centers if possible. The triangle, as it's known, was Jerusalem, Rome, and Santiago de Compostella in the north of Spain. Jerusalem and Rome are understandable, but Santiago is a bit of a different case. Legend says that St. James is buried there. (According to cold-blooded historical analysis, he probably isn't.) But the fact is that people thought that he was there even though his bones are not there. Traveling conditions were nothing like they are today and most of the trip would be done on foot. The Pilgrim's Road passed near Oviedo. In that area, the terrain is a very difficult mountain crossing, especially in winter, so travelers would detour to Oviedo. When pilgrims went to Oviedo, they wouldn't actually see the relics, only the oak chest where the relics were kept. The most they would be allowed to do is to touch one of the legs of the chest.

These pilgrimages led to the establishment of enormous French colonies all over the north of Spain and led to the building of churches, hospitals, and hostels where pilgrims could stay along the way. Places where travelers could buy food, shoes, and equipment also appeared. Going on a pilgrimage to Santiago was actually used as a legal punishment when some criminals were condemned to go to Santiago and back again. Many people didn't survive in the inclement season that they would encounter along the way. A rhyme in Spanish said that if a pilgrim went to Santiago, but not to Oviedo, he was visiting the servant, but not the Lord. Why? Because Santiago was where the apostle's remains were supposedly located, whereas Oviedo had the Lord's Sudarium. Therefore, many people considered it more important to visit Oviedo in their search to see relics from the passion. People still travel the Pilgrim's Road today, although the religious aspect has dropped out of the pilgrimages.

The Testing on the Cloth

The Sudarium is quite different than the Shroud of Turin. In John 20, we read how two disciples, the Beloved Disciple (John) and Peter, ran to the tomb on Easter morning after they heard that the tomb was empty. When they arrived, they saw the linen cloths lying on the rock. There have been all kinds of speculation as to the position of the cloths, but that speculation is unnecessary. The original Greek text is really quite clear about where each cloth lay. At least twice, if not three times, John writes that the face cloth was separate from the other cloth. That is perfectly compatible with the experiments that we've carried out on the face cloth.

Unlike the Shroud of Turin, the Sudarium has been studied extensively. The Spanish investigation team that worked on the cloth for years had complete access to it, so scientists have been able to do hands-on investigation as many times as they needed and whenever they requested. On investigating both the Sudarium and the Shroud, certain things are undeniable. It makes no difference if a person is a Christian, atheist, Muslim, or Buddhist, all the experiments carried out on the Sudarium are absolutely true apart from personal beliefs. The facts produced are purely scientific conclusions, and the results have been published in Latin, English, and Spanish.

The main stains in the middle of the cloth consist of 1 part blood and 6 parts plural edema fluid. This is explained by the fact that liquid collects in a person's lungs when he dies of asphyxiation. Other stains on the cloth correspond to the area of the back of the head. This is blood that was shed in life. This is also consistent with Christ's Crucifixion.

What is fascinating is comparing this cloth to the Shroud of Turin. If the cloths are overlaid or superimposed, the stains coincide in three areas. First, the blood group, AB, present on both cloths is the same. Second, the stains corresponding to the back of the head are blood that was shed in life on both cloths. Many of these little stains were caused by wounds from some kind of sharp object that penetrated the skin at the back of the head and made the person bleed while he was still alive. This is consistent with the crown of thorns. Third, by overlaying the images of the two cloths, the shapes of the blood stains coincide. All these facts lead to an inevitable medical conclusion that these two cloths were used on the same corpse. Whatever a person believes about the identity of the corpse wrapped in the cloths, science and medicine allow us to conclude that these two cloths covered the same body. The tests have shown too many coincidences between the two cloths for someone to say, "Well, the cloths were worn by two different people."

This leads to another conclusion. If the Sudarium covered the same corpse as the Shroud of Turin, then the Shroud is at least as old as the Sudarium. This finding is derived from medical science and is not influenced by any kind of religious belief or lack of it.

The Reproductions

Another type of experiment done on an exact replica of the Sudarium consisted of reproducing all the blood stains that are visible on the cloth. The stains on the replica have the same outlines as the stains on the original face cloth. The first stains dried before the next stains were formed. The experiments done on the cloth basically consisted of several rounds of experiments to reproduce the stains exactly as they are on the original. It took more than 6,000 attempts to get it right. In other words, we used the same fluid, 1 part blood 6 parts plural edema fluid, on a cloth that was exactly the same with a model head so that the angle of the head and the body could be measured. The only difference was the level in humidity between Madrid and the area around Jerusalem, but the effect of that on the times of drying the stains would have been quite minimal because they were done under laboratory conditions. These tests have been done in a laboratory a number of times, and the results have always been the same. This means that the results are not swayed by belief or even with lack of belief; this is pure science.

These experiments have shown us that human blood made the stains. The cloth must have been wrapped around the head of someone who was dead because the formation of these stains is incompatible with any kind of breathing movement where liquid came out through the nose and mouth. This mean that when people claim that Jesus didn't die on the cross but just swooned to be revived later in the tomb, the Sudarium tests show that this theory is not worth considering.

The main central stains were caused by a body that was in an upright position with the head leaning forward and to the right. The act of Crucifixion didn't require a body to be elevated high from the ground as long as the feet weren't touching the ground. One inch was enough, and that would have made things much easier for the Roman executioners and for those who were concerned about the body after his death.

From the pin holes in the cloth, we can see that the cloth was pinned to the back of the head, most likely during the Crucifixion. We carried out an experiment with the daughter of one of the scientists on the team who generously said that she would be the model. We covered her hair long hair with blood so that the hair became quite stiff and solid. When the cloth was pinned to the back of her hair, it held a pin without any problems. Our original idea was to wrap the cloth all the way around the head, but with rigor mortis setting in, the head was resting on the arm. Rather than lifting it up to wrap the cloth around it, stains show that the cloth was folded back on itself. Then the cloth was left on the upright body for between 45 minutes and 1 hour. During this time, liquid, blood, and plural edema fluid seeped out through the nose and mouth, leaving stains on the cloth. It took that long for these stains to form with the body in an upright position with the arms outstretched. That shows that the body was still on the cross when this cloth was first used on it.

The stains that caused the most problems to reproduce were the ones on the forehead. It took a long time to work out how they could have been formed. The only angle at which the staining could have occurred was with the body lying face down on the ground with the feet slightly higher than the head so that the liquid coming out through the nose and mouth would flow downwards and form the stains on the forehead. This was the only way that those stains could have been reproduced.

The Timeline

The tests allowed us to fill in a time line of what happened with this dead body in an almost minute-by-minute fashion. It was left in an upright position for between 45 minutes to an hour. It was then laid down, face on the ground with the arms still outstretched, most probably while it was still nailed to the cross beam, and left in that position for a further 45 minutes to 1 hour. At that point, the hands or the wrists were un-nailed and the arms were brought down to the side. The arm that was impeding the normal fold of the cloth was therefore no longer an obstruction. The cloth was then wrapped all the way around the head and tied in the knot at the top. The original linen still has the crease marks made from this knot. Interestingly, in a text from the third for fourth century, a paraphrase of the fourth Gospel by a writer named Nonas of Panopoles, speaks about the Sudarium having a knot tied in it.

At this point, the body was carried face down again for between 5 to 10 minutes, most probably when the two men took it to the tomb. During these 5 to 10 minutes, someone was holding the cloth tightly to the nose and mouth to absorb all of the liquid that was now gushing out of the nose and mouth because of movement from the lungs. A lot of liquid had collected in the lungs from the asphyxiation during the Crucifixion.

When the body reached the tomb, the face cloth was no longer needed. It was probably pulled off the head by holding the knot at the top. When it was lifted off the head, it was thrown to one side, which is how Peter and the Beloved Disciple described seeing the Sudarium on Easter morning.

All the tests point to the burial of Christ just as the Gospels portray it. We can take a further step and ask, "Since these cloths were used on the historical person of Jesus of Nazareth, what do you believe about that person?" This question has nothing to do with a professional, cold, scientific, and historical work. Each person must take this step inside himself and decide what the Sudarium means to him personally.

1988 CARBON-14 DATING PROVEN INVALID

by Alan D. Whanger, MD

On January 19, 2005, The American Shroud of Turin Association for Research (AMSTAR), a scientific organization dedicated to research on the Shroud, announced that conclusive evidence gathered over the past two years proves that the sample used to carbon date the Shroud in 1988 was taken from an expertly rewoven patch and not from the original fabric. The peer-reviewed studies proving this were done by chemist Raymond N. Rogers, a fellow of the Los

Alamos National Laboratory in New Mexico, and were published in the January 20, 2005, issue of the scientific journal *Thermochimica Acta*, pages 189-194. This article can be found at the website www.shroudstory.com.

The single sample that was removed from the Shroud in 1988 for radiocarbon dating was divided into several small samples, three of which were distributed to laboratories for testing. Rogers' research validates earlier observations by ourselves and others that the area from which the sample was taken appeared to be "invisibly" rewoven.

Our observations were based on high-resolution photographs both of the Shroud and of x-rays of the Shroud fabric, as well as on frames from the video of the taking of the sample for radiocarbon dating in 1988. When we first viewed this video and noted the abnormal threads extending into area from which the sample was taken, our immediate reaction was that the sample had been taken from a reinforced, repaired, or rewoven area and would give an entirely erroneous date. We were greatly distressed by this, as we had already been able to date the Shroud to the Spring of 30 AD by other means.

Samples of both warp and weft threads remaining from that single removed sample were given to Rogers for study in late 2003. In addition to the chemical testing of the threads themselves, he studied alternate methods for estimating the age of linen.

The most obvious change due to aging is the deepening of color as linen ages, but no correlation between color and age can be determined because bleaching methods have changed over the centuries.

Another indicator is the amount of vanillin present in linen fibers. The Holland backing cloth and other medieval linens gave a clear spot test for the presence of lignin (the phloroglucinol/HCL test for vanillin) on growth nodes, but fibers from the main body of the Shroud did not. This suggested that the rate of loss of vanillin from lignin could offer a method for estimating the age of the Shroud.

If the Shroud had originated between 1260 and 1390 AD as indicated by the Carbon-14 tests, lignin should be easy to detect, as linen produced in 1260 would still have about 37% of its vanillin in 1978 when the Shroud of Turin Research Project (STURP) testing of Shroud fibers was done. The lack of all traces of vanillin from the lignin in the Shroud indicates a much older age. No samples from any location on the main body of the Shroud showed the presence of vanillin. This is true also of the linen of the Dead Sea Scrolls and other very old linens. A determination of the kinetics of vanillin loss suggests that the Shroud is between 1300 and 3000 years old.

Rogers coupled these and other microscopic and microchemical observations with pyrolysis-mass-spectrometry results from the sample area to prove that the radiocarbon sample was not part of the original cloth of the Shroud. The rewoven fibers of the patch were so expertly dyed and rewoven that to the naked eye they appear to be part of the original fabric, but their chemical properties are completely different from the main part of the Shroud. These rewoven fibers were dyed using technology that began to appear in Italy about 1291 AD and was not in common use until more than 100 years later. Rogers said that the sample tested by the carbon dating laboratories couldn't be older than about 1290 AD, which agrees with the findings of the 1988 Carbon-14 testing.

Council for Study of the Shroud of Turin
www.shroudcouncil.org
Chairman, Alan D. Whanger, MD
P.O. Box 3190
Durham, NC 27715-3190

1988 Carbon-14 Dating of the Shroud of Turin Used Invalid Rewoven Sample

New Chemical Testing Points to Ancient Origin for Burial Shroud of Jesus

Dallas, TX—The American Shroud of Turin Association for Research (AMSTAR), a scientific organization dedicated to research on the enigmatic Shroud of Turin, thought by many to be the burial cloth of the crucified Jesus of Nazareth, has announced that the 1988 Carbon-14 test was not done on the original burial cloth, but rather on a rewoven Shroud patch creating an erroneous date for the actual age of the Shroud.

The Shroud of Turin is a large piece of linen cloth that shows the faint full-body image of a blood-covered man on its surface.

Because many believe it to be the burial cloth of Jesus, researchers have tried to determine its origin through numerous modern scientific methods, including Carbon-14 tests done at three radiocarbon labs (Arizona, Cambridge, and Zurich) which set the age of the artifact at between AD 1260 and 1390.

"Now conclusive evidence, as a result of Ray Rogers' thorough research, proves that the sample used to date the Shroud was actually taken from an expertly-done rewoven patch," says AMSTAR President, Tom D'Muhala. "Chemical testing indicates that the linen Shroud is actually very old—much older than the published 1988 radiocarbon date."

"As unlikely as it seems, the sample used to test the age of the Shroud of Turin in 1988 was taken from a rewoven area of the Shroud," as reported by the late chemist Raymond Rogers, a fellow of the Los Alamos National Laboratory in New Mexico. Rogers' new findings are published in the current issue of *Thermochimica Acta,* a chemistry peer reviewed scientific journal.[1]

---

1 [R.N. Rogers/*Thermochimica Acta*, Volume 425, Issues 1 & 2, pages 189–194, entitled "Studies on the Radiocarbon Sample from The Shroud of Turin," January 20, 2005].

"Pyrolysis-mass-spectrometry results from the sample area coupled with microscopic and microchemical observations prove that the radiocarbon sample was not part of the original cloth of the Shroud of Turin which is currently housed at the Turin Cathedral in Italy," says Rogers.

"The radiocarbon sample has completely different chemical properties than the main part of the Shroud relic," explains Rogers. "The sample tested was dyed using technology that began to appear in Italy about the time the Crusaders' last bastion fell to the Mameluke Turks in 1291 AD. The radiocarbon sample cannot be older than about 1290 AD, agreeing with the age determined in 1988. However, the Shroud itself is actually much older."

Rogers' new research clearly disproves the 1988 findings announced by British Museum spokesperson, Dr. Michael Tite, when he declared that the Shroud was of medieval origin and probably "a hoax." The British Museum coordinated the 1988 radiocarbon tests and acted as the official clearing house for all findings.

Almost immediately, Shroud analysts questioned the validity of the sample used for radiocarbon dating. Researchers using high-resolution photographs of the Shroud found indications of an "invisible" reweave in the area used for testing. However, belief tilted strongly toward the more "scientific" method of radiocarbon dating. Rogers' recent analysis of an authentic sample taken from the radiocarbon sample proves that the researchers were right to question the 1988 results.

As a result of his own research and chemical tests, Rogers concluded that the radiocarbon sample was cut from a medieval patch, and is totally different in composition from the main part of the Shroud of Turin.

FREQUENTLY ASKED QUESTIONS ABOUT DNA AND THE SHROUD

by Dr. Alan and Mary Whanger

Has DNA testing been done on the blood on the Shroud?

No authorized studies have been done. One study using an unauthorized sample yielded female DNA, not surprising since the Shroud has been mended several times by nuns and has been handled by countless persons over the centuries. Another test used samples too small for accurate testing which were extracted from dust vacuumed from the Shroud so that their exact location on the Shroud is unknown.

If not, why not?

There are two types of DNA. Nuclear DNA, the type usually referred to, is a huge molecule made of about 3 billion units called base pairs in a long twisted strand within the nucleus of each cell. It carries the genetic materials and directs the production of some 60,000 proteins that we need for life. The other type of DNA is found in the mitochondria, which are tiny bodies suspended in the cytoplasm of each cell and whose function is in metabolism and energy production. There are about 1,000 mitochondria in each cell, and each has a molecule of DNA made up of only about 16,500 units formed in a circle. Since there are about 1,000 times as many sources of mitochondrial DNA in a cell as nuclear DNA, testing for mitochondrial DNA is much more sensitive than for nuclear DNA when dealing with minute samples, although the potential information that could be found is much less.

Since there is no way to obtain blood from the person of Jesus for matching, what would be the significance of DNA studies if they were done?

If mitochondrial DNA studies of blood samples from the Shroud, the face cloth (Sudarium of Oviedo), and the seamless robe (Tunic of Argenteuil) all match, it would be strong evidence that these cloths all were in touch with the same body. This would be seen as confirmation of the traditional beliefs that these clothes were indeed in touch with the body of Jesus of Nazareth. Of course, all three cloths have been handled by many, many person over the centuries, hence the possibility of DNA contamination from other sources is high. But all three cloths have very different histories, and therefore have been handled by mostly different persons.

Have blood samples for DNA studies already been collected from these cloths?

In 1994, I (Alan) personally had the high honor of spending several hours painstakingly removing three sets of samples from the Sudarium of Oviedo. Each set consists of one thread from a blood-stained area and one thread from a nearby blood-free area to use as a control. These samples, which were carefully sealed and labeled, were removed for DNA testing, but they are stored in a freezer at the Spanish Ministry of Justice in Madrid awaiting approval for the testing to take place. For DNA testing of both the Shroud and the Tunic, new samples would need to be removed. Permission for this had not yet been granted.

We hear talk about the possibility of cloning a person. Could Jesus be cloned?
No, that is not possible. Theological considerations aside, in order to clone a living being it is necessary to have fresh DNA that is found in living cells and is not fragmented.

ATTEMPTED ATTACKS AND DESTRUCTION TO THE SHROUD

by Michael Minor

57 AD. Ma'nu VI, second son of Abgar V, succeeded to the throne of Edessa. Ma'nu reverted to paganism and cruelly persecuted Edessa's Christians. (The "portrait" disappears.)

1146 AD. Turkish Moslems captured Edessa. The city's historic churches, including Hagia Sophia Cathedral, were ruthlessly destroyed. However, the Mandylion remained safe in Constantinople within the Pharos Chapel.

April 12, 1204. Crusaders sacked Constantinople and destroyed buildings and church treasures. In the confusion the Mandylion/Sydoine disappeared. In de Clari's words: "... neither Greek nor Frenchman knew what became of it."

July 6, 1418. Due to danger from marauding bands, Lirey canons handed over the Shroud to Humbert de Villersexel for safekeeping. He received it in his castle of Montfort near Montbard. Later, it was kept at St. Hippolyte sur Doubs, the seat of the Counts de la Roche, in the chapel called des Buessarts.

December 4, 1532. Fire broke out in the chapel where the Shroud was kept at Chambery. The Shroud was removed to safety barely in time to keep it from being burned. The cloth was found to have had holes burned through it by molten silver from the melting reliquary.

1537 AD. Because of French invasions, the Shroud was taken for safety to Vercelli, Italy.

November 18, 1553. French troops sacked Vercelli. The Shroud was saved by one of the canons, Antoine Claude Costa, who hid it in his house.

1939 AD. The Shroud was taken to the Abbey of Monte Vergine (Avellino) for safety at the outbreak of World War II.

October 1, 1972. An attempt to set fire to the Shroud was made by an unknown person who broke into the Royal Chapel after climbing over the roof of the Palace. The Shroud survived due to the asbestos protection within the altar shrine.

Night of April 11–12, 1997. A mysterious fire of unknown origin broke out in the Royal Palace in the Turin, which spread to the Guarini Chapel, which is connected to both the Royal Palace and the Cathedral. It was an inferno inside the Guarini Chapel where the Shroud was housed. The Shroud was saved by the heroic efforts of the Turin firemen. Mario Trematore miraculously broke through a two-inch thick piece of bullet-proof and shatterproof glass to rescue the silver reliquary in which the Shroud was kept and, with great danger and difficulty, carried the almost four-foot reliquary to safety on his shoulders. When Trematore brought the Shroud out of the burning cathedral, he fainted, but he saved the Shroud.

AMSTAR
Michael Minor, Esq.
P.O. Drawer 878
Kaufman, TX 75142

BIBLIOGRAPHY

A

Adler, Alan PhD "The Nature of the Body Images on the Shroud of Turin." *Proceedings of the 1999 Shroud of Turin Research Conference.* Brian J. Walsh ed. Richmond, VA: Magisterium Press, 2000.

Anderson, Kerby. "Tales from the Crypt: Do We Have the Bones of Jesus?" American Family Association. Tupelo, KS. 28 February 28 2007. <http://www.afa.net>.

Antonacci, Mark. *The Resurrection of the Shroud.* New York: M.Evans & Company, 2000.

B

Behold A Mystery. Bershon, Paul, Dir. videocassette. Ariel Productions, 1991.

Bennett, Janice. *Sacred Blood, Sacred Image.* San Francisco, CA: Ignatius Press, 2005.

"Bones of Jesus Family, Canadian Documentary Claims," CBC News/ 2/26/07. <http://www.cbc.ca/world/ story/2007/02/26/Jesus-tomb.html.

Breault, Russ, Interview, *Shroud of Turin: Is It the Burial Cloth of Jesus?* DVD. Grizzly Adams Productions, Inc. 2000.

_____. "The Scientific Shroud." *Mysteries of the Ancient World.* Banbury, CN: Dell Publishing, 1995.

Brown, John L. Prof., Interview, *The Shroud of Turin: Is It the Burial Cloth of Jesus?* DVD. Grizzly Adams Productions, Inc. 2000.

Bucklin, Robert, Dr. ., Interview, *The Shroud of Turin: Is It the Burial Cloth of Jesus?* DVD. Grizzly Adams Productions, Inc. 2000.

C

Cameron, James. "James Cameron on Jesus." 26 February 2007. 27 February 2007 <http://www.msnbc.msn.com/ id/17349123>.

The Case for Christ's Resurrection. Sellier, Charles E., prod. DVD. Grizzly Adams Productions, Inc., 2007.

"Christian Scholars Poke Holes in Cable Documentary on Jesus Christ by Film Director James Cameron of 'Titanic." ASSIST News Service, Lake Forest, CA. 28 February 2007 <http://www.assistnews.net/>.

Colson, Chuck. "Sinking Credibility: The Media and the Bones of Jesus." Breakpoint with Chuck Colson. 1 March 2007 <http://www.breakpoint@wilberforce.org>.

"Cracks in the Foundation: The Jesus Family Tomb Story." University of the Holy Land. 27 April 2007. <http://uhl.ac?Lost_Tomb/CracksInThe Foundation.html.>.

D

De Nantes, Georges R.P., ed. "The Evidence of a Scientific Forger" *The Catholic CounterReformation in the XXth Century.* (March 1991:1-9).

D'Muhala, Tom, Interview, *The Fabric of Time*, DVD, David W. Balsiger, Senior Producer, Grizzly Adams Productions, Inc., 2006.

Driesbach, Albert Fr. "Did Peter See More Than an Empty Shroud?" Abstract. 1991.

_____, Interview, *The Shroud of Turin: Is It the Burial Cloth of Jesus*? DVD. Grizzly Adams Productions, Inc. 2000.

E

Erlich, Michael, Interview, *The Fabric of Time.* DVD, Balsiger, David W., prod. Grizzly Adams Productions, Inc., 2006.

F

The Fabric of Time, DVD, David W. Balsiger, Senior Producer, Grizzly Adams Productions, Inc., 2006.

Flury-Lemburg, Mechthild. personal conversation, May 6, 2006, Turin, Italy.

_____. *Sindone 2002.* Torino: Editrea ODPF, 2003.

Frei, Max, PhD, Interview, *The Shroud of Turin: Is It the Burial Cloth of Jesus*? DVD. Grizzly Adams Productions, Inc. 2000.

G

Garza-Valdez, Leonoccia, PhD, Interview, *The Shroud of Turin: Is It the Burial Cloth of Jesus*? DVD. Grizzly Adams Productions, Inc. 2000.

Guscin, Mark, Coordinator of Historical Investigation, Centro Espanol De

Sindonologia, Interview, *The Fabric of Time*, DVD, David W. Balsiger, Senior Producer, Grizzly Adams Productions, Inc., 2006.

H

Habermas, Gary R. *The Case for Christ's Resurrection*. Grand Rapids, MI: Kregel Publications, 2004.

———. Interview, *The Fabric of Time*, DVD, Balsiger, David W., prod., Grizzly Adams Productions, Inc., 2006.

Habermas, Gary R. and Licona, Michael R. *The Case for the Resurrection of Jesus*. Grand Rapids, MI: Kregel Publications, 2004.

Hanegraff, Hank. *Resurrection*. Nashville, TN: Word Publishing, 2000.

Heller, John, PhD, MD "Report on the Shroud of Turin." *Mysteries of the Ancient World*. Banbury, CN: Dell Publishing, 1995.

I

Iannone , John C. *The Mystery of the Shroud of Turin*. New York: Alba House, 1998.

J

Jackson , John, Dr. *Numismatist*. 1978.

_____. , Interview, *Behold a Mystery*, videocassette. Paul Bershon, prod. Ariel Productions, 1991.

_____. , Interview, *The Shroud of Turin: Is It the Burial Cloth of Jesus*? DVD. Grizzly Adams Productions, Inc. 2000.

Jacobovici, Simcha, and Pellegrino, Charles. *The Jesus Family Tomb*. San Francisco, CA: Harper Collins Publishers, 2007.

"Jesus Burial Site Discovery Is Just PR Spin," YNetNews. 25 February 2007. <http://www.YNetNews.com/article>.>.

L

Lynn, Donn, Interview, *The Shroud of Turin: Is It the Burial Cloth of Jesus*? DVD. Grizzly Adams Productions, Inc. 2000.

M

McCrone, Walter, PhD. *Judgment Day for the Shroud of Turin*. Amherst, NY: Prometheus Books, 1999.

_____, Interview, *The Shroud of Turin: Is It the Burial Cloth of Jesus*? DVD. Grizzly Adams Productions, Inc. 2000.

Miller, Lisa, and Joanna Chen, "Have Researchers Found Jesus Christ's Tomb?" *Newsweek*. 5 March 2007. 27 February 2007.

<http://www.msnbc.msn.com/id/17328478/newsweek>.

Minor, Michael, Interview, *The Fabric of Time*, DVD, David W. Balsiger, Senior Producer, Grizzly Adams Productions, Inc., 2006.

_____, Esq., "A Lawyer Argues for the Authenticity of the Shroud," *The Manuscript Society News*, 1990.

_____, Interview, *The Shroud of Turin: Is It the Burial Cloth of Jesus?* DVD. Grizzly Adams Productions, Inc. 2000.

_____, comp. *The Shroud of Turin: Unraveling the Mystery: Proceedings of the 1998 Dallas Symposium.* Alexander, NC: Alexander Books, 2002.

Mitchell, Dr. Edgar, Interview, *The Fabric of Time*, DVD, David W. Balsiger, Senior Producer, Grizzly Adams Productions, Inc., 2006.

Moran, Kevin, Interview, *Behold a Mystery*, Paul Bershon, producer, Ariel Productions, 1991.

_____, Interview, *Shroud of Turin: Is It the Burial Cloth of Jesus?* DVD, Grizzly Adams Productions, Inc. 2000.

Morison, Frank, *Who Moved the Stone?* Grand Rapids, MI: Zondervan Publishing House, 1930.

Muncaster, Ralph O., *Examine the Evidence,* Eugene, OR: Harvest House Publishers, 2004.

N

Nickell, Joe, Interview, *Behold A Mystery,* Bershon, Paul, Dir. videocassette, Ariel Productions, 1991.

_____. "The Shroud of Turin," *Mysteries of the Ancient World*, Banbury, CN: Dell Publishing, 1995.

P

Piczek, Dame Isabel, Interview, *The Fabric of Time*, DVD, David W. Balsiger, Senior Producer, Grizzly Adams Productions, Inc., 2006.

_____. Notes on the 3nd International Dallas Conference on the Shroud of Turin 2005 Symposium Paper.

_____. "The Professional Arts and the Principle and Practice of Conservation Restoration vs the Turin Shroud," *Proceedings of the 1999 International Research*

Conference, Brian J. Walsh ed., Richmond, VA: Magisterium Press, 2000.

_____, Interview, *Shroud of Turin: Is It the Burial Cloth of Jesus?* DVD, Grizzly Adams Productions, Inc. 2000.

_____. Taken from notes written May 2007 regarding the Interface Event Horizon.

Poirier, Jack, "The Statistics behind 'The Tomb,'" Jerusalem Perspective Online, 13 March 2007, 22 March 2007 <http://www. JerusalemPerspective.com.>

R

Ray Rogers, "In His Own Words," presented at the Dallas Shroud Symposium, 2005, Ray Roger's paper was published by Elsevier B.V. in *Thermochimica Acta* (2005), <http://www.elsevier.com/locate/tca> 189-194.

S

Scannerini, Silvano, *Myrrh, Aloes, Pollen and Other Traces*, Alan Neame, trans. London: St. Paul's, 1998.

Scavone, Daniel, PhD "The Scientific Shroud," *Mysteries of the Ancient World*, Banbury, CN: Dell Publishing, 1995.

_____., Interview, *Shroud of Turin: Is It the Burial Cloth of Jesus?* DVD, Grizzly Adams Productions, Inc. 2000.

_____. "Greek Epitaphoi and Other Evidence for the Shroud in Constantiople up to 1204."

Proceedings of the 1999 Shroud of Turin International Research Conference, Brian J. Walsh, ed. Richmond, VA: Magisterium Press, 2000.

Schumacher, Peter M., "Photogrammetric Responses From the Shroud of Turin," *Proceedings of the 1999 Shroud of Turin International Research Conference*, Brian J. Walsh, ed. Richmond, VA: Magisterium Press, 2000.

Schwortz, Barry, Interview, *Shroud of Turin: Is It the Burial Cloth of Jesus?* DVD, Grizzly Adams Productions, Inc. 2000.

Shermer, Michael, PhD, Interview, *Shroud of Turin: Is It the Burial Cloth of Jesus?* DVD, Grizzly Adams Productions, Inc. 2000.

Soons, Dr. Petrus, Interview, *The Fabric of Time*, DVD, Balsiger, David W., prod., Grizzly Adams Productions, Inc., 2006.

Stevenson, Kenneth PhD, Interview, *Shroud of Turin: Is It the Burial Cloth of*

Jesus? DVD, Grizzly Adams Productions, Inc. 2000.

Strobel, Lee, *The Case for Christ: A Journalist's Personal Investigation of the Evidence for Jesus,* Grand Rapids, MI: Zondervan Publishing House, 1998.

"A Summary of STURP's Conclusions," The 1978 Scientific Examination, 25 February 2007. <http://www.Shroud.com/78conclu.htm.>

T

Tite, Michael, PhD "The Scientific Shroud," *Mysteries of the Ancient World,* Banbury, CN: Dell Publishing, 1995.

————. Interview, *Shroud of Turin: Is It the Burial Cloth of Jesus?* DVD, Grizzly Adams Productions, Inc. 2000.

Thompson, Marshall, "Claims about Jesus' Tomb Stir Up Tempest," The Associated Press, 26 February 2007, 1 March 2007 <http://www.msnbc.msn.com/id/17345429>.

V

Vacarri, Albert, "Did Peter See More than an Empty Shroud?" Abstract, 1991.

W

Walker, Alison, *The Shroud of Turin: Unraveling the Mystery:* Michael Minor, comp, Alexander, NC: Alexander Books, 2001.

Whanger, Alan, Dr. *Flora of the Shroud of Turin*, St. Louis: MO: Missouri Botanical Press, 1999.

_____, Interview, *Shroud of Turin: Is It the Burial Cloth of Jesus?* DVD, Grizzly Adams Productions, Inc. 2000.

Whanger, Mary and Alan, *The Shroud of Turin: An Adventure of Discovery,* Franklin, TN: Providence House Publishers, 1998.

Wilson, Ian, Interview, *Behold a Mystery*, Paul Bershon, prod. Ariel Productions, 1991.

_____. *The Blood and the Shroud,* NY: The Free Press, 1998.

_____. "Highlights of the Undisputed History," *The Shroud of Turin: The Most Up-To-Date Analysis of All the Facts Regarding the Church's Controversial Relic,* Bernard Ruffin and C. Bernard Ruffin, Grand Rapids: Our Sunday Visitor, 1999.

_____. "The Shroud of Turin—Burial Cloth of Jesus Christ?" *Mysteries of the Ancient World,* Banbury, CN: Dell Publishing, 1995.

_____, Interview, *Shroud of Turin: Is It the Burial Cloth of Jesus?* DVD, Grizzly Adams Productions, Inc. 2000.

_____. "Urfa Turkey, A Proposal for an Archaeological Survey of the Town That was the Shroud's Home for Nearly a Thousand Years," *Proceedings of the 1999 Shroud of Turin International Research Conference,* Brian J. Walsh, ed. Richmond, VA: Magisterium Press, 2000.

Wolf, Dr. Fred Allen, Interview, *The Fabric of Time,* DVD, David W. Balsiger, Senior Producer, Grizzly Adams Productions, Inc., 2006.

Wolkowski, William, Dr. Professor of Physics at P.M. Curie University of Paris, *Written statement to Grizzly Adams staff, Dec. 30, 2005.*

Z

Zacone, Gian Maria, *On the Trail of the Shroud,* Alan Neame, trans. London: St. Pauls, 1998.

ABOUT THE AUTHORS

DAVID W. BALSIGER is a television producer-director, international rights supervisor, advertising executive, and the author of 40 major literary works including 25 nonfiction books. Additionally, he is the co-partner in Grizzly Adams Productions Inc. (named after the company's Grizzly Adams TV Series), the producers of family friendly and faith-based TV specials, series, and DVDs.

His most recent series for the PAX-TV Network (ION) was *Encounters with the Unexplained* (52 episodes), and a new series for syndication entitled *Xtreme Mysteries* (104 episodes). His other recent major TV/DVD specials include *The Case for Christ's Resurrection, Heroes Among Us, Miracles Around Us; Fabric of Time: Secrets of the Universe, Miracles in Our Midst, Apocalypse and the End Times, Breaking the Da Vinci Code, Faith in the White House, Miraculous Mission, The Evidence for Heaven, The Search for Heaven, Twelve Ordinary Men, Secrets of the Bible Code Revealed, Bible Code: The Future and Beyond, The Quest for Noah's Ark, The Bible's Greatest Secrets Revealed, The Bible's Greatest Miracles, Uncovering the Truth About Jesus* and *The Miracle and Wonder of Prayer*. He was also the director on the highly successful TV/DVD special entitled *George W. Bush: Faith in the White House*.

His well-known multimillion-copy best selling books *In Search of Noah's Ark* (Sunn) and *The Lincoln Conspiracy* (New American Library) have both been made into major movies of the same titles. He has also recently co-authored the books *The Case for Christ's Resurrection* (Bridge-Logos, 2007), *The Evidence for Heaven* (Bridge-Logos, 2005), *The Incredible Power of Prayer* (Tyndale, 1998), *Ancient Secrets of the Bible* (Dell, 1994), *The Incredible Discovery of Noah's Ark* (Dell, 1995), and *Face in the Mirror* (Bridge-Logos, 1993). Three of his previous books were million copy bestsellers including *The Lincoln Conspiracy, In Search of Noah's*

Ark, and *The Satan Seller*. His books, and video-TV projects have won more than 145 national awards for journalistic, literary, or production excellence.

He is listed in 19 achievement directories including eight of the prestigious Marquis library directories—*Who's Who of Emerging Leaders in America, Who's Who in Advertising, Who's Who in Religion, Who's Who in Entertainment, Who's Who in the Media and Communications, Who's Who in the West, Who's Who in America,* and *Who's Who in the World.* Mr. Balsiger is also the recipient of an honorary doctoral degree from Lincoln Memorial University (Harrogate, Tennessee) for his historical book *The Lincoln Conspiracy*□a 1977 book that was on the *New York Times* Best Sellers List for 22 weeks.

* * *

MICHAEL MINOR, a practicing attorney for thirty years, and former prosecutor, served for a number of years as General Counsel for the American Shroud of Turin Research Project, Inc., (STURP), the American scientific group which conducted extensive tests on the

Shroud of Turin in 1978. Minor currently serves as General Counsel and Vice President of the American Shroud of Turin Association for Research (AMSTAR). He has been involved in Shroud research for almost thirty years and has written several books, including *A Lawyer Argues for the Authenticity of the Shroud of Turin*. In Minor's book he argues that the circumstantial evidence favoring authenticity of the Shroud meets or exceeds the most stringent evidentiary requirement in a court of law "beyond a reasonable doubt".

Minor received his B. A. from Texas Christian University in Ft. Worth and his law degree from South Texas College of Law in Houston. He is listed in *Who's Who in the World, Who's Who in American Law* and *Personalities of the South*.

Minor is a fifth generation Texan and was born in Bowie, Texas.

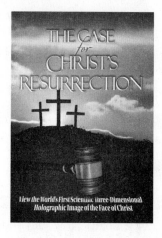

THE CASE *for* CHRIST'S RESURRECTION

EXECUTIVE PRODUCERS:
Vance Sphers, Paul Scvhubert, Joe Call

SUPERVISING PRODUCER: Charles E. Sellier

PRODUCER: David W. Balsiger

If it were a legal battle, it would undoubtedly be the most hotly contested case of all time. Did Christ really rise from the dead? Of all the world religions, only one—Christianity—claims that its founder rose for the grave. But is it true? Was Jesus' body really missing fro His tomb? Was Jesus seen alive after His death on the Cross? While Christians the world over accept by faith the validity of the Resurrection Story, there are just as many skeptics who demand proof. And like Jesus' own disciple, Thomas, they want to see the evidence for themselves.

How credible is the evidence for Christ's Resurrection? This documentary investigates the historical record, draws upon medical knowledge, searches for evidence in the lives of the Apostles, explores ancient Jewish burial customs, and, with new scientific technologies, examines the purported burial cloth of Christ. Your faith will be strengthened and your heart uplifted as the Resurrection Story is confirmed through new evidence!

Approximately 120 minutes including Bonus Features, plus FaithGrowers™ Curriculum and Pastor's Sermon Outline with Listener's Notes. DVD includes free three-dimensional viewing glasses.